SIXTY SELECTED
SHORT
NATURE
WALKS
IN CONNECTICUT

SIXTY SELECTED

SHORT NATURE WALKS

IN CONNECTICUT

Fourth Edition

by EUGENE KEYARTS

edited by CAROLYN BATTISTA

AN EAST WOODS BOOK

The Globe Pequot Press

OLD SAYBROOK, CONNECTICUT

Library of Congress Cataloging-in-Publication Data

Keyarts, Eugene.
  Sixty selected short nature walks in Connecticut / by Eugene
Keyarts ; edited by Carolyn Battista. — 4th ed.
      p.   cm.
    "An East Woods book."
    ISBN 1-56440-496-X
    1. Hiking—Connecticut—Guidebooks. 2. Connecticut—Guidebooks.
I. Battista, Carolyn. II. Title. III. Title: 60 selected short nature walks in
Connecticut.
GV199.42.C8K5   1994
796.5'1'09746—dc20   94-16610
                                               CIP

Contents

Middlesex County

New Haven County

New London County

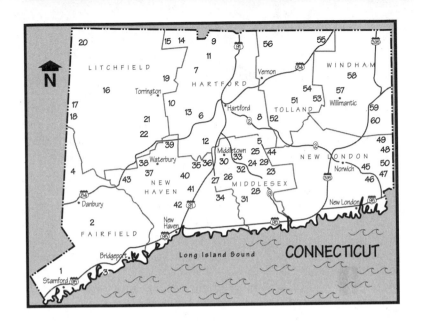

Tolland County

Windham County

Trail Information

After you have walked some or all the trails listed in *Short Nature Walks in Connecticut* you may want to try some other trails.

There are thousands of miles of walking trails throughout every state in the nation. You will find them in all national parks and in many state forests and state parks. For information write to the Conservation Department in the state you are interested in.

For information about the Connecticut Blue Trails, write to:
Connecticut Forest and Park Association
16 Meriden Road, Route 66, Middlefield
Middletown, CT 06457
(Connecticut Walk Book)

For other information about Connecticut trails, nature centers, and walks, write to:
State of Connecticut
Bureau of Outdoor Recreation
State Parks Division
Department of Environmental Protection
79 Elm St., Box 5066
Hartford, CT 06102–5066

Appalachian Trail Conference
Box 807
Harpers Ferry, WV 25425

Appalachian Mountain Club
5 Joy Street
Boston, MA 02108

Adirondack Mountain Club
Connecticut Valley Chapter
c/o Arthur Potwin
128 Shingle Mill Road
Harwinton, CT 06791

For Topographic Maps to supplement trail maps, write:
U.S. Geological Survey
Washington, DC 20242

Introduction

Who hasn't wished to escape, if only for a few hours, the pressures of modern living? Who hasn't wanted to get away from the hustle and hurry, away from the crowd, to go on foot into the woods and fields?

Should you be of the opinion that open space and natural areas are not available due to our state's dense population, then you are in for a pleasant surprise.

Connecticut is second to none in what it has to offer the hiker—woods, farmland vistas, lakes, streams, rolling hills, and abundant wildlife. Many think that the most beautiful sights are hundreds of miles away, that it is necessary to leave our state and drive frustrating miles, battling week-end traffic snafus, to view scenes that are no better and perhaps inferior to those within our own boundaries.

The Connecticut Forest and Park Association maintains more than 500 miles of cleared and well-marked woodland trails throughout the state, and many of the walks in this book are on these trails. They are known as the Connecticut Blue Trail System, and they touch every county of the state. You can reach from your home the most distant of these trails within a few hours, with plenty of time to explore the trail, spend a picnic hour in pleasant surroundings, then return home at a leisurely pace to sleep in your own bed that night.

Each section of the blue-blazed trails has something unique to offer. Some of the most picturesque scenery in all New England may be seen on these walks. Nature lovers, be their interests trees, flowers, minerals, caves, or just exercise, will find much to gratify them on these walks.

This guide's primary objective is to inform those nature lovers of varied tastes just where they may pursue their interests freely without the restrictions of NO TRESPASSING signs.

It is possible that some would prefer more details on things of special interest to be found along the trails. Detailed descriptions of things, unless outstanding, are not given because we feel the wider general interest would not be served. What is of prime importance to the rock hound may have little appeal to the botanist, and not all bird watchers will be impressed by ferns or trees.

This guide contains sixty short walks. The walks are compiled according to the county they are in, so that a resident of a particular county may first select those walks nearest his or her home.

The sketch maps for each walk are not according to scale but are intended to show the relationship of the trail to roads and other landmarks and to clarify the written directions.

The 500 miles of the Connecticut Blue Trail System are not for the sole use of hiking clubs or the dyed-in-the-wool hiker. The trails are there and maintained for your use and pleasure as well. Perhaps you are not a member of a hiking organization, yet would like to take your family afoot to commune with woods and waters. If so, these short walks in Connecticut on the blue-blazed trails—and in a few other spots—are for you.

Special Note

Change is the rule of nature; but her changes are slow, barely perceptible, and usually beneficial. Man, on the other hand, makes drastic changes to solve immediate problems, only to create more harmful situations for himself in the future.

Due to man-made changes—superhighways, crowded developments, and shopping complexes—we continue to destroy acres and acres of irreplaceable natural areas.

Since disruption and change is inevitable, we can only suggest that the user of this guide accept and comply with all trespass regulations. In many instances, however, a polite request of the property owner for permission to follow a trail over private land is usually granted.

the trees, wildlife, and wildflowers that inhabit the different sites. An interesting feature is a sturdy boardwalk winding through the swamp and bog areas.

Members of the arboretum staff are constantly working on and offering varied programs of interest to the novice and expert alike. Tours will be conducted by appointment. It is requested that the appointments be made at least one week in advance. For arrangements and/or further information, contact the arboretum office by telephone, or write: The Bartlett Arboretum, 151 Brookdale Road, Stamford 06903.

It is not necessary to take a guided tour. Individuals or small groups may roam the grounds on their own. To the student of nature there is something of interest taking place at all times and in every season at the arboretum. If any season may be considered superior, it has to be spring.

The poet Henry Van Dyke wrote, "The first day of spring is one thing, and the first spring day is another. The difference between them is sometimes as great as a month."

Whether spring is on time or comes a bit late, it is a period of anticipation and fascination. The skunk cabbage pushes up a tentative probe but is careful to keep her cowled hood tightly closed. The red-winged blackbird suddenly announces his arrival, sounding his cheery unmistakable *tee-er-ree* call while clinging to a swaying upright reed. When the bloodroot and shadbush flaunt their white blossoms and the yellow adder's-tongue cautiously appears, spring is truly here.

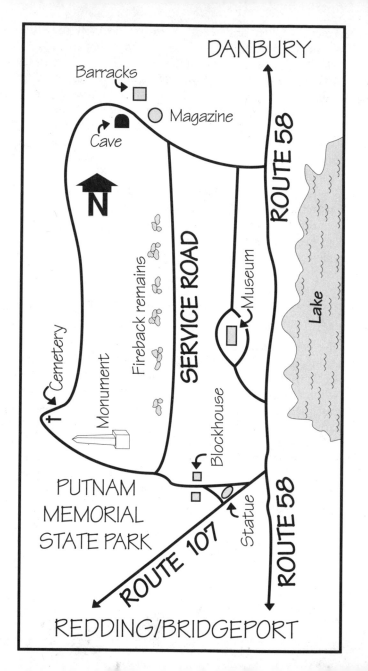

2

Putnam Memorial

This is not so much a walk on leaf-strewn trails as it is a meander through some early leaves of American history. The Putnam Memorial State Park in Redding, Connecticut, has been dedicated to memorialize the site of the winter encampment of the right wing of the Continental Army during the winter of 1778–79.

This historic state park comprises some 230 acres of land and includes one of the best preserved winter campsites of the Revolutionary War period. In this area between eight and nine thousand troops suffered through that cold, stormy winter. General Washington's encampment during the previous winter at Valley Forge may have received more publicity, but the hardships endured by the men of the Redding encampment were equally severe.

Israel Putnam was the senior major general of the Continental Army at the time of the winter encampment at Redding. He was affectionately called "Old Put" by his men. It was he who persuaded the army leaders that this base at Redding was militarily and strategically the most logical.

The British were entrenched in New York, and they continued to harass the state of Connecticut. The previous year the soldiers of King George III had attacked and burned Danbury, a major army supply depot. From the Redding encampment, Old

Put contended, his men could defend the heart of Connecticut. They could help to defend the southeast Connecticut coast, the western Connecticut area, and also be prepared to return to the Hudson River in the event of an attack.

To reach the Putnam Memorial, follow the most convenient routes to the junction of Route 107 with Route 58 in the township of Redding. The entrance to the campground is directly west of the junction and is dominated by a larger-than-life bronze equestrian statue of the general. It depicts him making good his dramatic mounted escape from pursuing British dragoons down the perilous one hundred steps carved into the precipice at Horse Neck, Greenwich, in 1779.

The main gate is flanked by two high blockhouses guarding the gateway. Passing through the gate, you then ascend to the crest of the hill, where an obelisk made of native granite and measuring 10 feet square at the base and 40 feet in height, crowned by a cannonball 2½ feet in diameter, is located. On the face of the monument is the following inscription—ERECTED TO COMMEMORATE THE WINTER QUARTERS OF PUTNAM'S DIVISION OF THE CONTINENTAL ARMY NOVEMBER 7, 1778–MAY 25, 1779.

The memorial shaft is at the beginning of the actual campground, which is studded with mound after mound of rock piles. These are the fallen chimneys and walls—or firebacks—left where they tumbled from the soldiers' huts.

There is much of historic interest here, including a reconstructed guard house, the 12-by-16-foot log huts that housed twelve men, officer's hut, Phillips' Cave, cemetery, and powder magazine.

A visit to the museum is a must. You may drive the service roads to get a quick overall view; then park your car and wander afoot to the various points that may be of interest to you.

Sherwood Island

Connecticut has many firsts to her credit, among them Sherwood Island State Park in the township of Westport. Established in 1914, it was the first state park in Connecticut and one of the first state parks in the nation. It is composed of 234 acres of sandy beach, marshes, groves of linden and maple trees, picnic facilities, and a spacious modern pavilion. The park's major feature is its long sweeping beach bounded on the south by Long Island Sound.

The park was named in honor of the Sherwood family, who were early settlers here after migrating from England's Sherwood Forest, where Robin Hood and his band of followers allegedly gave the sheriff of Nottingham the run-around.

The entrance to Sherwood Island State Park may be reached by following the most convenient route to Exit 18 of the Connecticut Turnpike, Route I–95, in Westport. From Exit 18 turn south onto the Sherwood Island Connector and follow .6 of a mile to the park gatehouse; then park your car in the designated area.

One may take the Westwood Nature Trail, or just wander leisurely along the 1.25-mile-long beach, through the groves, and over the marshes. Winter is the ideal time for the hiker to visit this park—one is apt to find it deserted or at most with only a handful of visitors. This is also the best season to observe wintering waterfowl and other sea birds.

Since it is better to walk with a purpose than to meander

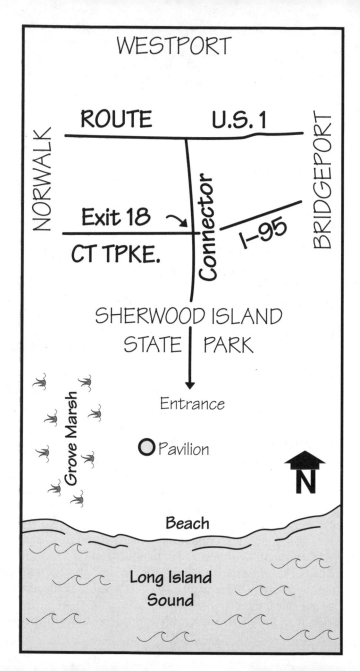

aimlessly, this walk should start at the far eastern end of the park's beach. Walking close to the water's edge as it ebbs and falls to low water can be a fascinating experience.

Exploring the shoreline as you go, continue west on the beach to a fence at the western end of the park. Turn right, leaving the beach, to enter a picnic grove on higher ground. The grove rises a few feet above the surrounding marsh; this higher ground provides an exceptional observation post for bird watchers. When conditions are favorable, and with proper footwear, the marsh may be investigated with caution.

After the walk you may wish to go on to the roof deck of the pavilion for a panoramic view of the park grounds, Long Island Sound, and, on a clear day, Manhattan skyscrapers. Should the weather be too blustery to picnic comfortably at an outside table, there is a protective glass screen on the pavilion's lower level. This mammoth picture window provides a pleasant outlook to the sound and also affords unexpected warmth when the sun shines through it.

Rachel L. Carson wrote in *The Edge of the Sea*, "Wherever land and sea meet--along a sandy beach, against a rocky shore, across a mud flat or at the edge of a coral reef--a weird and wondrous array of plants and animals exists in a turbulent world that can be breathtakingly beautiful and at the same time unyieldingly harsh."

Our New England shoreline does not have the exotic sea life found near a coral reef. But the temperate zone's less colorful algae, seaweed, barnacles, mussels, clams, and other marine life struggling to survive are of the utmost importance to the ecology and chains of life found here.

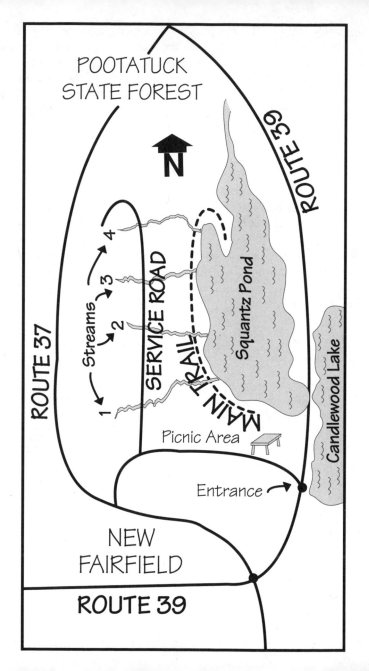

Squantz Pond

Of all the state's parks, Squantz Pond in the Pootatuck State Forest is second to none in setting, beauty, and facilities to suit every taste. The main attraction is the pond itself, with sandy beaches for the children and deeper waters for stronger swimmers. One may also fish, boat, water ski, picnic, hike, or just relax.

Squantz Pond is an arm of unique and beautiful Candlewood Lake, the largest body of water within the state. Candlewood Lake was man-made for water power to generate electricity. Here is proof that man can with care and thought alter nature's pattern for his utilitarian purposes without destroying the beauty, naturalness, and usefulness of an area.

The entrance to Squantz Pond State Park is off Route 39 in the town of New Fairfield. Approaching from the south at the intersection of Routes 37 and 39, New Fairfield, turn north onto Route 39 and follow 3.8 miles to the entrance. From the north, at the junction of Routes 37 and 39 in Sherman, take Route 39 south approximately 6 miles to the park entrance west of the highway.

Enter through the gate and park your car in a designated area. The hiking trails are on the west side. The main trail starts at the north end of the picnic area and follows the edge of the pond's western shoreline. The trail and side trails are not blazed but are so worn and well defined that one may follow them easily.

Keeping close to the water's edge, go north to the first of four major streams splashing down several hundred feet from the mountain above to the pond below. Crossing the stream, follow the main path along the pond bank, always bearing right.

There are many side trails leading away from the pond, and these may be explored as you desire. Though the trails are not blazed to guide you, there need be no fear of getting lost. The pond is always visible, and one has only to walk toward the water to pick up the main trail paralleling the shoreline.

Before investigating any of the side trails, it would be advisable to stay on the main trail past the other two streams, the last of which is about 1½ miles from the picnic area. From the third stream the trail is less trodden but nevertheless visible and easy to follow to a small peninsula with an unobstructed view of the entire pond. The peninsula is approximately 2 miles from your starting point and is an ideal spot to rest before returning to your car.

The trail is strewn with huge boulders tumbled helter-skelter from the high and massive rocky ridge that rises almost directly from the pond's edge to a height of more than 400 feet.

Depending on the amount of time and energy you have to spend, explore the streams and side trails, where there are numerous caves to be found.

Squantz, for whom the pond is named, was a chief of the Pootatuck Indians, who once hunted and held sway over these bountiful mountains and valleys. Folklore would have us believe that Paul Bunyan also roamed these hills, for there is much talk about blue oxen and incredible feats performed by mighty loggers with double-bitted axes.

5

Salmon River State Forest and Gilead Area

The Gilead block of the Salmon River State Forest is located in the township of Marlborough. This area is known as excellent bird cover, especially in the vicinity of the Blackledge River.

This segment of state forest also offers good hiking terrain. There are no blazed trails, but Woods Road leads through delightful upland hardwood forest with small coniferous plantations, a few brooks, and wetland areas.

This inviting bit of forest is easily reached from the east or west via Route 66. Approaching from the east, drive to the intersection of Routes 66 and 85 in the township of Hebron. From the intersection follow Route 66 west 3.1 miles to the Hebron-Marlborough boundary line; continue .8 mile to a woods road on the right. Approaching from the west, drive to the intersection of Routes 2 and 66 in Marlborough. From the intersection follow Route 66 east 1.5 miles to Blackledge River. The woods road is a short distance east, on the north side of Route 66. There is ample parking space inside the north guard rail.

From Route 66 follow the woods road north to a three-way intersection of forest roads. (If you continue right on Slocum, it becomes a paved road.) Returning from this intersection the round-trip will be about 3 miles.

Near this walk is the Eastern District Headquarters of the

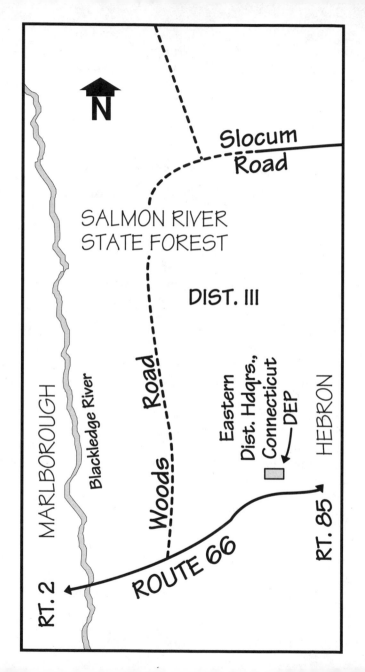

Connecticut Department of Environmental Protection. Visitors are welcome here during working hours, Monday through Friday. Maps and literature on Connecticut parks and forests are available.

Only after most deciduous trees have dropped their leaves do we become aware of growth deformities on trees, shrubs, and other plants. These unusual, but not uncommon, grotesque growths are known as galls. Although galls have been loosely referred to as a sort of plant cancer, plants rarely die or suffer serious injury from them.

Galls are abnormal plant structures that develop after an insect has deposited her eggs on or in a plant. When the egg hatches, the larva lives, feeds, and grows to maturity within a gall built by an unwilling host and used as a cradle, pantry, and citadel by the uninvited freeloading guest.

From earliest times the gall was used as a food, in medicine, and in commerce. The gall's most valuable contribution to man is the large amount of tannic acid derived from it.

Entomologist Charles T. Brues, author of *Insects, Food, and Ecology,* gives us an interesting sidelight on galls: "To mankind in general, especially to the literary, legal and educational professions, in fact all those who use ink, or misuse it, to preserve the written word, the gall insects have unwittingly made their greatest contributions. For more than a thousand years certain galls have formed a major ingredient of the best and most permanent writing inks."

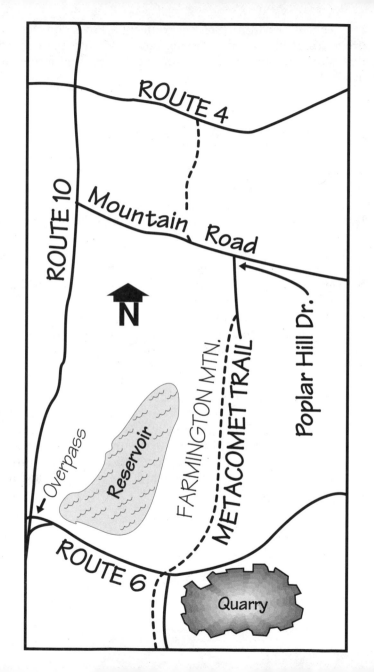

6

Farmington Mountain

One is led to wonder what was being offered free in 30 B.C. when the Roman poet Virgil said, "I fear the Greeks, even when bringing gifts."

There is never a need to be skeptical about the free gifts of nature. Her offerings are always sincere and direct, never in pettifogging small print. To base the worth of nature's gifts by what they cost is a false criterion.

Nature offers much to the walker on the Blue Trails of Connecticut, all at a minimum cost. One of the state trails that will reward the hiker generously at slight cost is the Metacomet Trail as it passes over Farmington Mountain in Farmington.

This section of the Metacomet starts with the rock cut on Route U.S. 6 at .9 mile east of the Route 10 overpass. The trail crossing Route 6 is indicated by blue blazes. Park your car on the south side of the highway, not on the television company's private road.

Follow the trail north to the ridge, passing several towering hemlock patriarchs guarding the trail gateway. At the top of the rise, a fine view of the quarry operation across the highway is to be had, as well as an impressive sight of the television tower spiring above the peak of Rattlesnake Mountain. From the western edge of the ridge, Farmington Reservoir may be seen 250 feet below. A few outlooks along the ridge present good views of "Farming-town" to the west.

Continue on the blazed trail in a northeasterly direction to Poplar Hill Drive. The trail follows Poplar Hill to Mountain Road, jogs left on Mountain Road for .2 mile, then enters woods and passes the property of the Hill-Stead Museum as it continues to Route 4. This stretch from Route 6 to Route 4 round-trip is about 3 miles. Use your own judgment as to how far in you wish to go before returning to your car. You may wish to use the two-car system should you go from road to road; leave one car on Route 4, the other on Route 6, then walk from car to car. You should note that Route 6 and even Mountain Road are trafficky. Take care crossing.

This area offers a variety of mature forest trees common to our state. You will find oaks, hemlocks, beeches, birches gray and white, pines, and many others. If you have been identifying trees by their leaves, you might wish to try your skill at naming trees after they have taken off their summer dress, in fall or winter.

Unless you are expert at this you may find it difficult at first. There are many fine guides to help the novice name a tree by its bark, twigs, and fruit. Three guides that I have found most useful are *Trees of the Eastern United States* and *Fruit and Twig Key to Trees and Shrubs,* both written by William M. Harlow and published by Dover Publications; and *The Natural History of Wild Shrubs and Vines* by Donald W. Stokes, published by The Globe Pequot Press. These are paperbacks, economical and handy to carry in pocket or knapsack.

Playing games with nature is much more rewarding and gratifying than all the games of bingo, pinball, lucky bucks, or sweepstakes that man may devise. Man's bait soon loses its tempting allure, but nature's offerings will never pall.

7

Firetown Trail

The 4,500-acre McLean Game Refuge is the legacy of George P. McLean, who wanted the meadows, woods, and streams of the refuge "to be seen by those who love them as I love them." Its features include picnic areas, one of the Barndoor Hills, and 20 miles of trails.

Firetown Trail is an interesting trail in the western area of the refuge. It may be walked in two or three stages; one particularly lovely section starts from Firetown Road in Simsbury and leads to the West Ledge Trail, where there are several old cellar holes.

To reach the starting point of this walk, drive to the entrance of McLean Game Refuge, 1 mile south of the intersection of Routes 10 and 20 in the township of Granby. From the entrance, follow Route 10 south .2 mile to Canton Road. Turn right onto Canton Road and follow it 1.8 miles to the County Road intersection where Canton Road leads into Holcomb Road. Follow this southwest .9 mile to Barndoor Hills Road, and continue on Holcomb Road .4 mile to the Firetown Road intersection. Turn right onto Firetown Road and follow it 1.4 miles to the blue-blazed Firetown Trail crossing.

Park your car where the trail comes in on the right; then follow the blazes along the road to where the trail reenters the

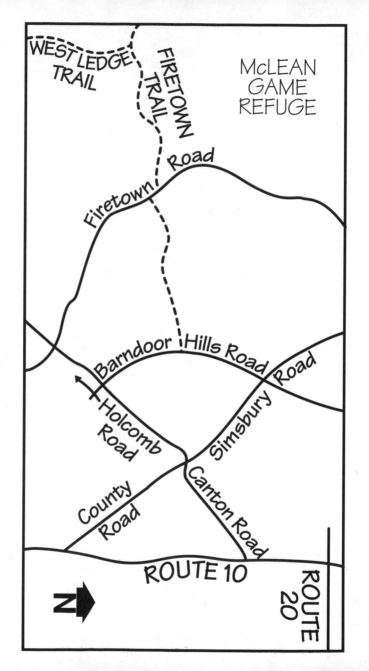

woods, on the left. Follow the blazed trail west .2 mile to the juncture with West Loop Trail, entering from the right. Keep left on the main trail, paralleling the brook. After crossing the brook, the trail continues on the woods road to the juncture with West Ledge Trail, on the left, 1 mile from your car.

Turn left onto West Ledge Trail and ascend a hill, reaching old cellar holes in .7 mile. From here you may head back to your car.

Visitors to the refuge are asked to not take or disturb anything around these cellar holes. Like hundreds of other such holes on trails, woods roads, and abandoned town roads throughout Connecticut, they are all that remain of once comfortable, snug farmhouses.

Most of these foundations were laid up without the use of mortar. Many of these homesites are more than one hundred years old, but the stone cellar walls remain surprisingly sound and intact, bespeaking skilled workmanship.

Of first importance in these cellars were a large bin for the storage of potatoes and barrels for pie and eating apples. Carrots were kept in layers of sand, turnips and parsnips were piled on the floor. Cabbages with roots attached were suspended from overhead floor joists, as were smoked hams and slabs of bacon. Wall shelves were lined with tier upon tier of mason jars packed with last summer's bounties.

Some households had their yearly compromises. Mother was granted space for her unpotted geraniums and dahlia bulbs, and father was permitted to roll in two barrels of apple cider—provided he allowed one to turn into vinegar.

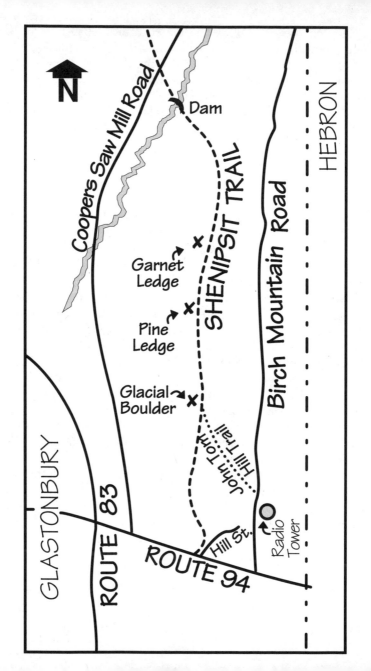

Glacial Boulders

All of Connecticut was covered with a vast sheet of ice during the glacial period. The evidence of the great glacier's action is to be found everywhere in the state. An interesting deposit of glacial boulders may be found on the Shenipsit Trail in the town of Glastonbury.

For the starting point of the trail portion that passes through the glacial boulder area, drive to the intersection of Hebron Avenue (Route 94) and Hill Street (a dirt road). This intersection is 2.7 miles east of the intersection of Routes 94 and 83; it is .1 mile west of the intersection of Route 94 and Birch Mountain Road, which is 2.4 miles west of the intersection of Routes 85 and 94. (You can park along Hill Street, but be sure not to block this one-lane road.)

The blue-blazed Shenipsit Trail heads north on Hill Street, then enters the woods on the left at .14 mile. It follows an old tote road along the edge of a field and climbs gradually to the top of a ridge at .34 mile. It then continues through the woods (passing under power lines at .53 mile), and at .75 mile reaches a large glacial boulder and a trail junction. The area is strewn with boulders of every size and variety.

(At the junction, the John Tom Hill Trail, marked with red and blue, goes to the right. This side trail will descend steeply, cross a brook, go under the power lines, and continue through woods to reach Birch Mountain Road, .44 mile from the junction and .1 mile north of a radio tower.)

The Shenipsit Trail descends from the boulder-strewn ridge to a swamp and a tote road just north of the swamp. From the tote road, the trail ascends gradually and then steeply for a short distance to Pine Ledge, with a fair view to the west. Leaving Pine Ledge, the trail descends through a sag before climbing to the top of Garnet Ledge, almost 2 miles from the start of the walk. The ledge was so named because it and many of the boulders are studded with tiny garnets.

The round-trip to Garnet Ledge is less than 4 miles. Should you wish to go farther, you may follow the self-guiding trail northwest to an old dam, then to Roaring Brook, before reaching Coopers Sawmill Road, less than 3 miles from the start.

As you walk this trail, you will become aware that, even though you appear to be on high ground, you are actually completely surrounded by much higher hills. Very likely the crags and rugged peaks of the surrounding mountains were bulldozed by the gigantic mass of ice, which then held the rough rocks in its grasp for centuries, grinding and shaping them into the forms in which we now see them. As the ice sheet melted, the captive mellowed stones were released many miles from their origin.

It is estimated that these boulders were dumped in this area approximately 20,000 years ago. All of Connecticut was drastically changed by the work of the great glacier.

Geologists guess that the ice at its peak was more than 1,000 feet thick over New Haven and that it exerted a pressure of 50,000 pounds per square foot on everything it passed over.

Its advance and retreat obliterated old land and rivers, creating new lands and bodies of water. Thanks to the work of the glacier, our state is blessed with a total of 1,026 lakes and 420 swamps.

9

Manituck Lookout

The blue-blazed Metacomet Trail follows a traprock range running from Meriden to the Massachusetts line. The Indian after whom it was named, Metacomet, was also called King Philip.

The section of the trail south of Route 168 has fine outlooks along a 2-mile stretch that begins at Phelps Street in the town of Suffield.

Phelps Street is on the west side of Route 168 about 3 miles east of Congamond Lake. The juncture of Phelps Street with Route 168 is 2.1 miles west of the intersection of Routes 168 and 187 in West Suffield.

Park your car in the vicinity of Phelps Street. Follow the blue-blazed trail west on Phelps Street for .1 mile to where the blazed trail leaves the road to the left (south). Scramble up a steep slope to a woods road and follow the road till it reaches a traprock ridge affording fine views.

A little more than a mile into the walk, Manituck Lookout looks down on Manituck Mountain, a flat-topped rock mass directly to the west.

The trail passes through the Suffield Conservancy and a town park, then reaches a traprock crag, Chimney Point, from where the Barndoor Hills and the Western Highlands come into view.

Should you decide to return to your car from here, the round-trip will be approximately 4 miles. Or you may decide to follow

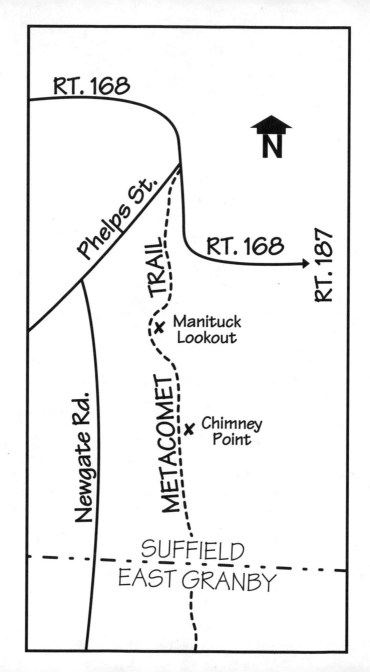

the self-guiding trail south a little further before returning to the starting point.

Other than beneficial exercise, some may question the value of walking in the woods during the winter season. The woods in winter seem devoid of life, but one finds what one looks for.

It is not easy for many of us to appreciate the significance of the commonplace. Our feeling toward the familiar is too often the too common attitude—so what?

How little thought we give, if any, to the blanket of leaves crackling underfoot as we stride along a trail. Yet how tremendously important is this commonplace layer of leaves in nature's overall plan.

The vast annual crop of leaves dropped on the earth is a more valuable harvest than that of any grain or seed. Fallen leaves are not dead. They still live in the soil, which they enrich in depth and fertility each year, if only by a leaf's thickness. Shedding their leaves, the trees and shrubs repay with interest what they borrowed earlier. Nothing really dies or is lost in nature; decay is but a new form of life, a reincarnation.

Thoreau had this to say about fallen leaves: "It is pleasant to walk over beds of rustling leaves. How beautifully they go to their graves. How gently lay themselves down and turn to mold. They that soared so loftily, how contentedly they return to dust again and are laid low, resigned to lie and decay at the foot of the tree and afford nourishment to new generations . . . as well as to flutter on high. They teach us how to die. One wonders if the time will ever come when men with their boasted faith in immortality will lie down as gracefully and as right."

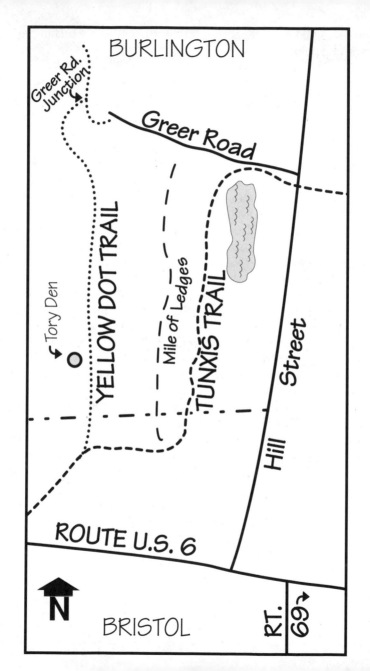

Mile of Ledges

The Tunxis Trail offers many attractions as it meanders over miles of pleasing woodland terrain, among them one of the steepest miles to be found on the Connecticut Blue Trail System, historic Tory Den, and Devil's Kitchen Ravine. Not the least of them is the Mile of Ledges, alleged to be the roughest part of the southern Tunxis Trail.

The Mile of Ledges is on the Tunxis in the township of Burlington. To reach the starting point of this walk, follow the most convenient route to the city of Bristol's combined Route U.S. 6 and Route 69. From Route 69 at the western end of the combined routes, follow Route U.S. 6 west 1.1 miles to Hill Street. Turn north, right, onto Hill Street and follow it 3 miles to Greer Road. Turn northwest, left, onto Greer Road and follow .2 mile to the western edge of a large pond, where the trail leaves the road to enter woodland. Park your car and follow a blazed trail south over undulating terrain ascending gradually to the Mile of Ledges. At about .5 mile from Greer Road, you will encounter one towering ledge after another for the next half-mile before reaching the Yellow Dot Trail, which is blue-blazed with a yellow dot in its center.

At the junction of the main blue-blazed Tunxis Trail with the Yellow Dot Trail, turn north, right, and follow the Yellow Dot Trail to historic Tory Den, about .2 mile. Tory Den is an historic landmark; it was used as a hideout during the Revolutionary War by the Tories of the area when too hotly pressed by overzealous Patriots. Today the Den continues to offer sanctuary, peace, and solitude to those who would flee momentarily the pushing press of civilization.

From Tory Den the Yellow Dot Trail continues north just over a mile to Greer Road Junction. Turn right, descend to Greer Road, and follow the road approximately .5 mile to your parked car.

When walking the woodland trails during any season except winter, it is probable that one or more bumblebees will be seen. Whether you call these bees bumble or humble, either is correct, but bumble is most common. Both names suggest the humming, buzzing, droning sound made by these insects when in flight. The scientific name of the genus is *Bombus,* Latin for "buzzing" or "humming."

The bumblebee has a large black body covered with a thick fuzzy coat of white or yellow hair. Its flight is not so graceful as that of the honeybee, yet it maneuvers expertly in flight. A scientist, after examining a bumblebee, declared that aerodynamically, due to its large body, clumsy design, and small wing surface, it could never take to the air. Fortunately for man, the bumblebee does not know the rules, so miraculously she flies.

We owe much to the bumblebee for her services as a pollinator of plants we need. Those flowers with deep corollas, which cannot be reached by the short-tongued honeybee, must be served by the longer-tongued bumblebee.

The bumblebee is a social insect, but, unlike honeybees, the bumblebee colony does not live over winter; only the young pregnant queens survive, coming out of hibernation in the spring to start a new colony.

Peak Mountain

The highest point on the Metacomet Trail between Tariffville and the Massachusetts state line is Peak Mountain. It is 672 feet above sea level, with exceptional views. The mountain may be easily reached from either Route 190 in Suffield or Route 20 in East Granby. The shortest approach is from Route 20 on the south.

To reach this point, follow the most convenient route to the intersection of Routes 20 and 187 at East Granby. Follow Route 20 west .6 mile to Newgate Road, on the right. On Route 20 near the corner is a standard blue and white oval sign indicating the Metacomet Trail. The walk to Peak Mountain starts here.

Park your car on Newgate Road and follow the trail north up a very steep wooded slope. The trail continues north on the crest of the ridge, with fine views to the east and west. Much of the trail is marked with the green blazes of the East Granby Land Trust. Peak Mountain is reached 1 mile from Route 20. Descending the north face of Peak Mountain at about .1 mile, there is a side trail that leads down the mountain's west slope .5 mile to Newgate Prison. This side trail is difficult to find, as it is heavily overgrown and poorly blazed at its juncture with the Metacomet Trail.

From the Newgate Prison side trail, the main trail leads north along the crest of Peak Mountain through hardwood forest to

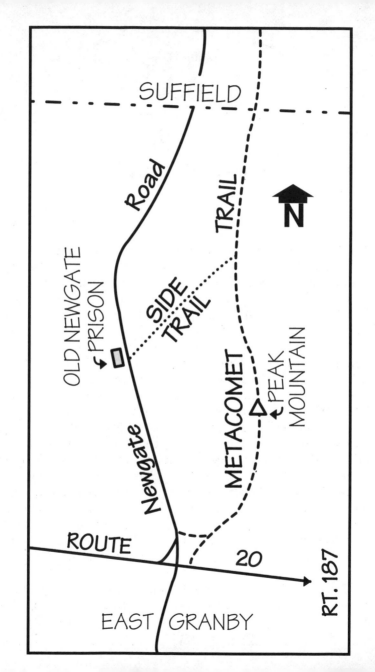

SUFFIELD

Road

TRAIL

N

OLD NEWGATE ←PRISON

SIDE
TRAIL

Newgate

METACOMET

←PEAK
MOUNTAIN

ROUTE

20

RT. 187

EAST GRANBY

Turkey Hills Lookout, at approximately 1.3 miles from the starting point.

You may wish to rest and picnic here while enjoying the distant views. The round-trip from this point will be 2.6 miles. Return from here or, should you desire to go farther, continue on the blazed trail north, returning from any point you decide upon.

There is an extra bonus that may be enjoyed together with this walk to Peak Mountain. This section of the Metacomet Trail parallels Newgate Road, on which Newgate Prison is located. It is only 1.2 miles north from Route 20 to the crumbling remains of what was once a busy copper mine and later a state prison and a federal jail.

Old Newgate Prison is the property of the state. It is open to the public as a site of historic interest. Its history began in 1705, when it was known as Copper Hill and the first mining probe for copper was started. In 1707, a group of land proprietors of Simsbury formed the first company to work the mines.

In 1773, the Colony of Connecticut first used the tunnels and caverns 30 feet below the surface as a permanent prison. It was during the American Revolution that the title of the prison was changed to Newgate after Newgate Prison of London, England. In 1781, Congress made Newgate of Connecticut a government jail for prisoners of war. During its fifty-four years as a prison, many British, Tory, and state prisoners were kept in the dank, dark dungeons. As many as forty prisoners at one time were confined in the rock-hewn holes, and they were compelled to work in the mine and workshops. In the 1820s, female prisoners were sent to Newgate, but they were kept in cells above ground.

After 1824, when Wethersfield was made a state prison site, Old Newgate Prison was abandoned.

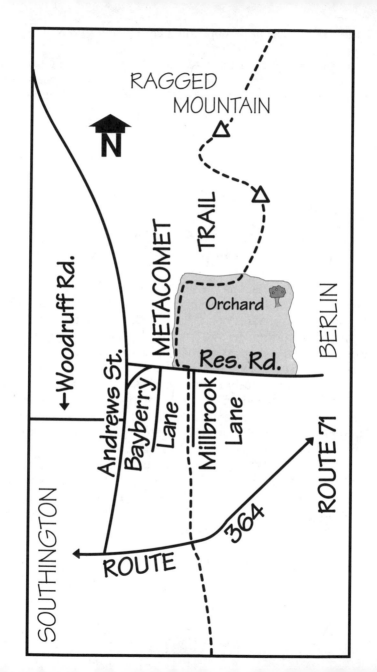

12

Ragged Mountain

No matter what your special interests may be, if you enjoy walking in the woods, trees cannot help but intrigue you.

We must agree with Sam Walter Foss when he says, "Oh, bare must be the shadeless ways and bleak the path must be, . . . Of him who, having open eyes, has never learned to see. . . . And so has never learned to love the beauty of a tree."

Every species of tree has its own distinct story. One such species we are apt to encounter on these short walks in Connecticut, especially on the rocky ridges, is the chestnut oak. It is also called mountain oak or rock oak and has acquired these names from its leaf, which resembles that of the chestnut, and from its fondness for rocky or mountain ridges.

The chestnut oak is mainly a mountain tree of the Appalachians. It may attain a height of 100 feet on favorable sites, but it is so wind-whipped on the exposed ridges of Ragged Mountain that it usually is stunted and twisted, resulting in a tree with a trunk that frequently divides into several angular limbs, making an open, irregular-shaped head. The wood is hard, strong, and close-grained. Its bark is dark reddish-brown, thick, and deeply divided into broad, rounded ridges. These oaks are of great ecological benefit in that they prevent erosion of soil that barely supports other vegetation.

An unusual concentration of chestnut oak trees is to be found atop and on the slopes of Ragged Mountain, located in the towns of Berlin and Southington.

Ragged Mountain is a geological feature of the two towns. Their common boundary line skips from high point to high point across the mountain's crest. The Metacomet Trail crisscrosses this line as it ascends and descends.

To reach this section of the trail from Southington, take Route 364 east. In approximately 3 miles, Route 364 turns onto Kensington Road. In another .5 mile, turn north on Andrews Street. Follow Andrews Street about 1 mile to the junction with Woodruff Road; continue on Andrews Street .4 mile to a fork, bear right, and drive about .5 mile to Bayberry Lane.

Or, from Route 71 (near the junction of 71 and 71A) in Berlin, turn west onto Reservoir Road and drive approximately 1.5 miles to Bayberry Lane.

On the north side of Reservoir Road, across from Bayberry Lane, is a parking area. The trail to the mountain begins there, following a road, then entering the woods just past utility pole #4264. The trail is clearly blazed, well trodden, and easy to follow.

Climb steeply to an excellent view from first overlook; continue north and west to the summit of Ragged Mountain, at an elevation of 754 feet.

With open eyes, there is much to be seen and enjoyed following the blue-blazed Metacomet Trail over Ragged Mountain.

13

South Talcott Mountain

Connecticut is the fourth most densely populated state, yet many of its 3,212,000 acres are undeveloped. The urban and built-up areas of the state take up only 603,000 acres; the rest is cropland, pastureland, or forest. Since we live and work on such a small percentage of the land, it is not surprising that many of us get that crowded feeling from the tensions of modern daily living.

Former Secretary of the Interior Stewart L. Udall once stated, "It may be that, in the long run, overpopulation in this country will threaten the most important freedom we enjoy . . . the freedom each person must have to maintain his own integrity, to discover his natural self and be true to it."

The Connecticut Forest and Park Association has from its inception endeavored to provide and conserve for us the state's public lands: parks, forests, trails, waters. The association long has realized that each person must have elbow room and an opportunity for occasional solitude.

One solution to the problem has been the establishment of the Blue Trail System, where one may escape, for a short time at least, from the complexity of urban and suburban living.

Through the efforts of many state agencies you, as a state resident, are part owner of a vast domain. This land is your land, scattered generously throughout the state, some of it per-

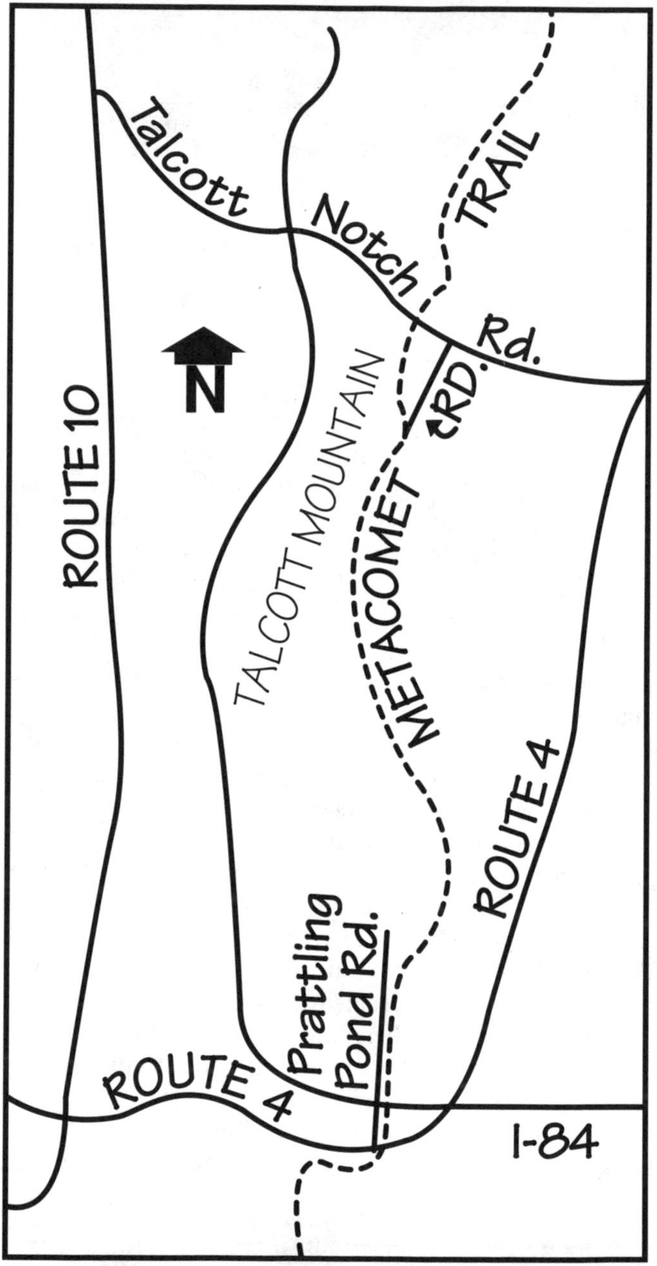

Talcott Notch Rd.
N
ROUTE 10
TALCOTT MOUNTAIN
METACOMET TRAIL
RD.
ROUTE 4
Prattling Pond Rd.
ROUTE 4
I-84

haps only a short distance from your doorstep. Go out and inspect and enjoy your holdings.

You may start on any one of the numerous blue trails that comprise the 500 miles of the system. Start if you wish on an interesting section of the Metacomet Trail that passes over the south end of Talcott Mountain in the town of Farmington.

At exactly 1 mile east on Route 4 from the intersection of Routes 4 and 10, the Metacomet Trail turns north onto Prattling Pond Road. To reach this road, be sure to go east on Route 4; avoid going straight onto Route I–84. Park your car off the traveled portion of Route 4 (or use the commuter parking lot across Route 4). Prattling Pond Road is a private road; a wooden post, with blazes on the back stands at its northeast corner.

Follow Prattling Pond Road north about half a mile to where the trail enters the woods toward the east and continues along old woods roads and bushed trail in a northerly direction. At 1.1 miles, the woods road reaches paved Metacomet Road and follows it briefly. The trail then reenters woods and reaches Talcott Notch Road at 1.4 miles. For a short walk this may be a good place from which to return to your car, the round-trip being slightly more than 3.5 miles.

Although we have been preaching, "This land is your land," it is also the other fellow's; we share it with others. When using the trails, remember that many of the state's adjoining holdings are reached by crossing private property. We naturally are obligated to respect the generosity of these landowners who allow us to use and cross their property by leaving the trail improved or in the same condition in which we found it.

When using state or private land, a considerate hiker never leaves trash, even when unobserved. A good trail motto is "Take only pictures, leave only footprints."

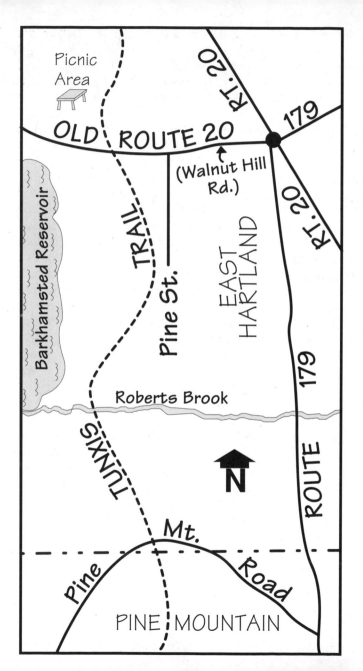

Roberts Brook

The Tunxis Trail passes through the township of Hartland between and paralleling the Barkhamsted Reservoir and the Hartland–Granby boundary line. Roberts Brook is crossed by the trail approximately 1.75 miles south of old Route 20 and about .75 mile north of Pine Mountain in Barkhamsted.

To reach this walk, drive to the intersection of Route 20, Route 179, and Old Route 20 (Walnut Hill Road) in East Hartland. Follow Old Route 20; about 1 mile from the intersection, keep following Walnut Hill straight into the forest while Pine Street goes off to the left. About .25 mile into the forest, the blue-blazed Tunxis trail crosses the road; this walk starts on the left side of the road. (For a walk heading in the opposite direction, see Walk 15.)

Park your car and follow the self-guiding trail south, ascending immediately to a crest. The trail dips and rises over several hills and shortly reaches a barbed wire fence on the west, which it clings to it some of the way. Use care when following this trail; there are deceptive paths and woods roads that tend to lead one astray. Be sure to have a blue blaze in view before advancing too far.

Roberts Brook is reached at just under 2 miles. The trail continues south for about .75 mile to Pine Mountain Road and the north base of Pine Mountain. You may return to your car after reaching Roberts Brook or extend your walk by going on to Pine Mountain for a fine view of Springfield before returning.

Winter is a time to be enjoyed, a period to be accepted with zest, not aversion. There is as much pleasure to be found on snow-covered trails as at any other season of the year.

Henry David Thoreau advised us, "Live each season as it passes; breathe the air; drink the drink, taste the fruit, and resign yourself to the influence of each. Let them be your only diet, drink, and botanical medicines. Be blown on by all the winds. Open all your pores and bathe in all the tides of nature, in all her streams and oceans, at all seasons."

He gave us similar advice, though a little less flowery, when he wrote, "Take long walks in stormy weather or through deep snows in the fields and woods, if you would keep your spirits up. Deal with brute nature. Be cold and hungry and weary."

Winter is no longer considered a bore, an annoyance to be endured, as attests the explosive interest displayed by skiers, snowmobilers, snowshoers, and winter hikers. We no longer envy those who follow the sun. If we think of them at all it is with commiseration for what they are missing.

People are only now becoming aware of what plants, animals, and birds have always known—that snow is to be lived in with appreciation. Snow is as welcome and essential as the sun and the rains to most living things. It acts as insulation against the wind and cold, offering a warm shelter to most of nature's creatures.

When a deep layer of snow has accumulated, mice, shrews, and weasels build runways and little cities under the snow, which offer protection against freezing temperatures. Snow is so constituted that life-giving air seeps in easily while cold penetrates it slowly.

Bear in mind that, while extremely enjoyable, winter hiking is far different from summer hiking. Do not take preparation for even an afternoon's outing lightly, and always travel in company. Winter in the woods is an experience to be shared.

An excellent "how-to" is *Winterwise* by John Dunn, published by the Adirondack Mountain Club.

15

Tunxis State Forest

At the northern end of the Tunxis Trail, near its terminus at the Massachusetts borderline, are some exceptionally fine walks. One of the most rewarding is the segment between Old Route 20 and Route 20 in the township of Hartland. The entire walk, all within the boundaries of the Tunxis State Forest, is less than 5 miles long, round-trip.

To reach this walk, drive to the intersection of Route 20, Route 179, and Old Route 20 (Walnut Hill Road) in East Hartland. Follow Old Route 20 straight into the forest (approximately 1 mile from the intersection, Pine Street goes off to the left). About a quarter of a mile into the forest, the blue-blazed Tunxis Trail crosses the road; this walk starts on the right side of the road. (For a walk heading in the opposite direction, see Walk 14.)

The trail soon crosses a delightful brook, then continues on a service road a short distance before descending smartly to another brook flowing into Barkhamsted Reservoir. After crossing the brook, the trail ascends gradually to a dirt road and turns right, east; it follows the road briefly, then turns left, north, and follows an easy path to reach Route 20 at approximately 2 miles from starting point.

Returning from here, retrace your steps to the dirt road, where the trail reenters the woods to the left, south. The dirt road was at one time the approach to a ski slope, once popular

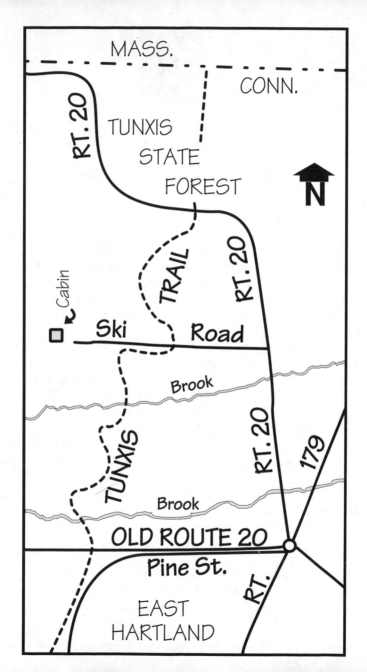

but now abandoned. The road is now used only as a part of an occasional cross-country ski run and as an approach to a large cabin at its western end.

The log cabin, state-owned, is at the dead end of the dirt road about .25 mile west of the blue-blazed trail crossing. Although the cabin is off the main trail, a side trip to visit it will prove an extra bonus. Leave the south leg of the trail and follow the road west to the site of the cabin. This is an ideal spot to picnic and rest. Returning from the site, follow the road east to the blazed trail, then back to the picnic area and your car.

The present sections of the Tunxis State Forest were probably never occupied or controlled by the Tunxis Indians, who were a subtribe of the Sicaogs. Grand Sachem Sequassen ruled both tribes. The Sicaogs claimed the area that is now Hartford and West Hartford, while the Tunxis tribe settled in the Farmington area, including much of the surrounding lands.

The Indian name for the Farmington River was *Tunxis*, which is an abbreviation for *Tunxisepo*, also *Tunchseasapose*. Both of these forms are abbreviations of *Watunkshausepo*, which means "fast-flowing and winding river." It is supposed to have described the sharp bend in the Farmington River where its flow changes abruptly from a southeasterly to a northerly course. It was quite natural that the tribe living in the Farmington River Valley became known as the Tunxis Indians.

What is now known as the Tunxis State Forest was in all probability a part of the land in the northwest corner of Connecticut never permanently settled by any Indians. This was a sort of no-man's-land constantly fought over by the Mohawks of New York and the Tunxis of Connecticut, both claiming this rich hunting ground as their own. This dispute continued until the white man took over.

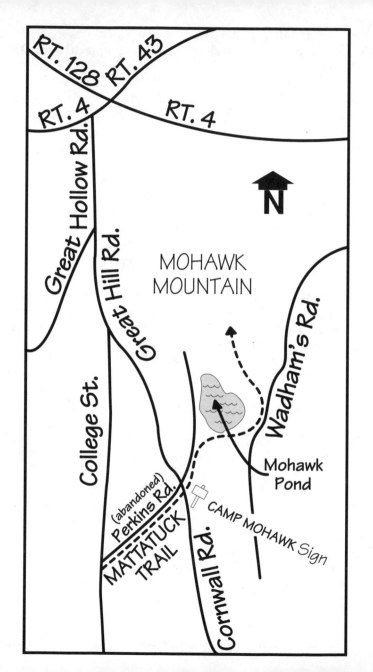

16

Mohawk Mountain

Mattatuck was the Indian name for the intervale between Waterville and Naugatuck. The blue-blazed Mattatuck Trail is approximately 35 miles long; its longer southern section is separated by about 13 miles of road from the shorter northern section. In the Mohawk State Forest in Cornwall, a beautiful segment of the northern section skirts Mohawk Pond and climbs Mohawk Mountain.

Follow the most convenient road to the junction of Routes 4, 43, and 128 in Cornwall. From the intersection, follow Route 4 west .1 mile to Great Hollow Road. Turn left, south, onto Great Hollow Road and follow it 1.8 miles to Great Hill Road. Bear left on Great Hill to College Street at .9 mile. Bear right on College Street; follow College 1.3 miles to an abandoned road and Mattatuck Trail, leading northeast.

Park your car, being careful not to block driveways or woods roads. From College Street, head northeast on (abandoned) Perkins Road. Cross the road at 1 mile and follow Camp Mohawk Road, which turns right at 1.4 miles and heads toward Mohawk Pond. Continue parallel to the east shore of the pond, then veer away from the pond and out to (dirt) Wadhams Road. Continue north along this forest road, then turn left into woods to ascend Mohawk Mountain to its summit (1,680 feet), about 3 miles from College Road. Enjoy the view before beginning your descent.

When Ralph Waldo Emerson asked, "What is a weed?," he answered his own question. "A plant whose virtues have not yet been discovered."

The commercial virtues of the weed commonly known as Queen Anne's lace have yet to be discovered. The plant is also known as bird's nest and wild carrot. It is believed to be the stock from which the garden carrot was raised. The botanists have classified it as *Daucus carota*, a member of the parsley family. Farmers unanimously classify it as the "peskiest" of weeds.

During the months of August and September we are apt to see an abundance of the plain white, symmetrical, perfectly formed, circular flowers of the wild carrot that appear like so many miniature lace doilies enhancing the appearance of our roadsides. Queen Anne's lace has one supreme virtue—simple beauty.

17

River Road

The 50-mile stretch of Appalachian Trail in Connecticut is mostly steep and rugged terrain. In contrast there are a few sections of this trail that are more or less level and relatively easy to walk. One such section is the 5-mile stretch on the west bank of the Housatonic River between St. John's Ledges in Kent and Silver Hill in Sharon.

To reach the base of St. John's Ledges, where this walk begins, drive to the intersection of Routes U.S. 7 and 341 in the center of Kent. From the intersection follow Route 341 west across the Housatonic River Bridge to Skiff Mountain Road. It is the first road to the right west of the river. Turn north onto Skiff Mountain Road and follow 1.1 miles to the junction with River Road. Skiff Mountain Road bears left here. Follow it until it forks with a dirt road on the right. Take the dirt road (not maintained in winter) and continue 1.7 miles to the Appalachian Trail crossing, indicated by white blazes.

Park your car and follow the white-blazed trail north as it parallels or follows River Road. Trail and road cling close to the river on the east. (If you wish to avoid walking on the road, you can drive to a parking area at the end of River Road, about a mile past St. John's Ledge, and take the trail as it enters the woods.)

Numerous streams tumble down the face of the mountain range and flow into the Housatonic in this area. The river and the mountain streams along this portion of the Appalachian Trail

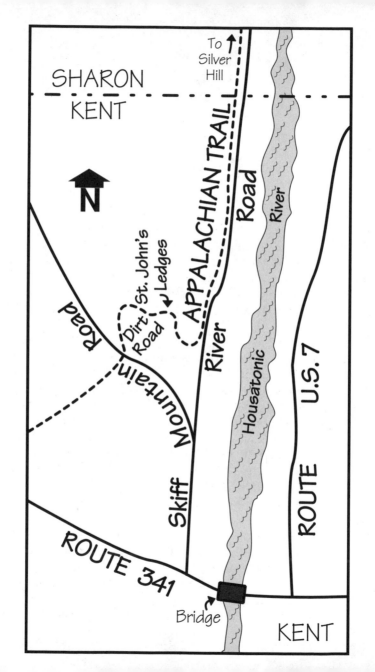

have an eye-appeal unmatched by sights from higher elevations.

The river walk continues for about 5 miles to Silver Hill. (There the trail goes on up the hill, then descends sharply.) You may walk the entire distance or shorten your walk to whatever length you wish.

When nature dominates the scene, our streams, rivers, and natural areas are things of beauty. Nature's ways are always beneficial and harmonious.

When man interferes selfishly, we have ugliness and chaos. Man has befouled most of his living space: air, land, and water. His wanton killing of animal life has made hundreds of species extinct. He has indiscriminately and wastefully used natural resources beyond reclamation—all in an effort to accumulate so-called wealth.

Like fabled King Midas, man has succeeded so well in turning everything he touches into gold that now, almost too late, he is discovering that one cannot live by gold alone.

Why does man have this devilish drive, urge, and unholy skill to destroy or damage almost everything he comes in contact with? Nature's method is not to destroy beyond recall but rather to provide food chains for survival and balance.

One creature that has been able to survive not by destroying but rather by benefiting the things she touches is the honeybee. She has survived for over nineteen million years; upstart man is but an infant born yesterday by comparison. The honeybee has perfected a successful society whose sole needs are nectar, pollen, and propolis. All these needs are supplied by plant blossoms as an inducement for the bee's services, without which the plants could not perpetuate themselves.

The honeybee may outlive man another nineteen million years unless he learns from her that the lesson of survival is doing, serving, and giving rather than taking.

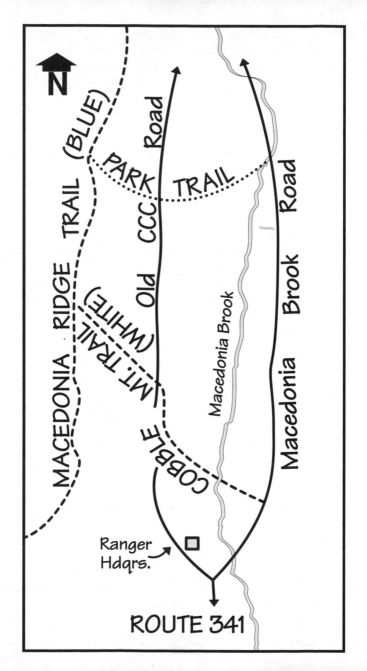

N

MACEDONIA RIDGE TRAIL (BLUE)

MT. TRAIL (WHITE)

PARK TRAIL

Old CCC Road

COBBLE

Macedonia Brook

Macedonia Brook Road

Ranger Hdqrs.

ROUTE 341

18

Cobble Mountain

Macedonia Brook State Park is in the town of Kent. Cobble Mountain, on the Macedonia Ridge Trail, is the highest point (1,380 feet) in the area.

The park has a variety of trails, from easy through moderately stiff to rugged. Here you may take a leisurely stroll or a strenuous all-day hike. There are several loop trails of varying lengths that bring you back to the starting point without retracing your steps. One of these is the white-blazed trail leading to Cobble Mountain.

Macedonia Brook State Park's south entrance may be reached from the intersection of Routes 7 and 341 at the center of Kent. From this intersection drive northwest on Route 341 approximately 1.7 miles to Macedonia Brook Road, which is the main road through the park. Turn north onto this road and follow it to the park entrance, indicated by the sign. About 1 mile from the entrance, the Ranger Headquarters is located between Macedonia Brook Road and the old Civilian Conservation Corps Road, once called Sharon Road, on the left (west).

The white-blazed trail begins on Macedonia Brook Road. It is marked by a sign saying COBBLE MOUNTAIN where it crosses a footbridge near the pavilion just north of the Ranger Headquarters. After parking your car, follow the white-blazed trail northwest, ascending steeply for .4 mile to the juncture with the blue-blazed

Macedonia Ridge Trail. Follow the blue-blazed trail west (right) to the crest of Cobble Mountain. The view from here is extensive and magnificent. It is one of the finest outlooks in the state.

Spend as much time as you wish on the mountain top, and when satiated follow the blue-blazed trail .3 mile to the juncture with the green-blazed Pine Hill Trail, which descends south another .3 mile to CCC road, thence south on the CCC road .4 mile to the starting point.

The blue-blazed trail comes down from the mountain over rough and rugged terrain. Although the hazardous portion of this trail is short, it should be negotiated with care. It is advisable not to try this section when it is wet or covered with snow. Under these conditions do not try the green-blazed trail. It would be better to retrace the white-blazed trail back to your car.

Macedonia Brook State Park, composed of 2,294 acres, has an abundance of all those things that appeal to naturalists. Whether your interest is geology, botany, wildlife, hiking, or just a desire for quiet and solitude, you may satisfy it here.

Macedonia Brook flows through 4 miles of picturesque gorge in the heart of the park in Nodine Hollow. The main road passes through the park from Route 341 on the south to the Sharon-Kent boundary line on the north. All but one of the trails start from the main park road. Those to the east are generally less steep than those to the west.

Each trail is blazed with its own color: white, red, yellow, blue, green, or orange. A map showing the various trails and other features may be obtained from the ranger on duty. In season, the picnic and campsite areas in the park are very popular. For those who wish to get away from the crowd, winter is the ideal season to visit.

19

Mount Ratlum

Mount Ratlum is on the Tunxis Trail of the Connecticut Blue Trail System near the midpoint of Ratlum Road, which begins in New Hartford and ends in Barkhamsted.

Approaching from the south and west, follow the most convenient route to the intersection of Routes U.S. 44 and 219 in New Hartford. From the intersection follow Route 219 east 1.5 miles to Ratlum Road in the township of New Hartford.

Approaching from the east, drive south to the junction of Route 179 with Route 219 in Barkhamsted. From the junction follow Route 219 southwest 1.5 miles to the north end of Ratlum Road, in the township of Barkhamsted; continue on Route 219 approximately 3.75 miles to the south end of Ratlum Road, in New Hartford.

The New Hartford Ratlum Road terminus is about 100 feet north of Richard's Corner Dam at the south end of the Compensating Reservoir. Turn northeast onto Ratlum Road, passing Ski Sundown and following blue blazes on trees along the road until the blazed trail enters the woods.

Park your car and follow the blazed trail north, ascending easily to Mount Ratlum, less than 1 mile from the starting point. Be sure to sign the trail register. Then enjoy the outstanding views of the valley to the north, the Compensating and

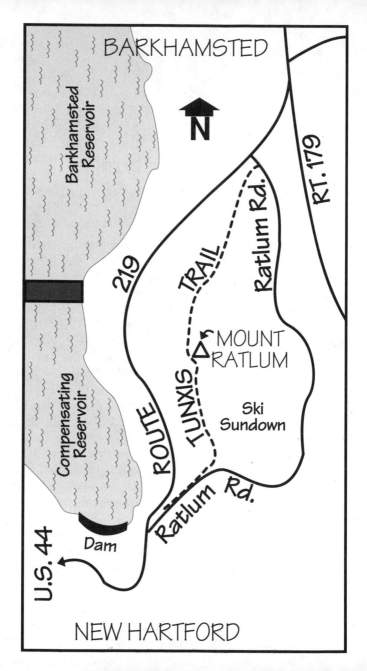

Barkhamsted reservoirs, and the East Branch of the Farmington River. In season, you can see skiers riding up the lifts and zooming down the slopes of Ski Sundown.

The trail continues north from Mount Ratlum 2.5 miles to the Barkhamsted terminus of Ratlum Road. The round-trip from one Ratlum terminus to the other is approximately 7 miles. You may do all of it or return from Mount Ratlum or any other point along the trail you desire.

The hiking enthusiast who puts his knapsack, shoes, and other gear in storage as soon as snow begins to fall is missing one of the better times of the year to follow woodland trails. Most year-round hikers agree there is no such season as best.

In winter there are no insects; it is easier to dress comfortably for cold weather than hot; there is no foliage to block near and distant views; and snow tracks tell interesting stories. Trying to interpret wildlife tracks in the snow can add another dimension to the woods walker's experiences.

To most animals, snow may prove to be both an asset and a liability. The quality and quantity of a snowfall may be the difference between life and death for predator and prey. A light crust on deep snow may help a small animal escape from a floundering pursuer. A snow-covered pile of brush offers small animals shelter from the cold and safety from predators. To man, a blanket of snow is usually considered a nuisance, a threat to his comfort, or a seasonal novelty. At best it is a thing of beauty to be enjoyed.

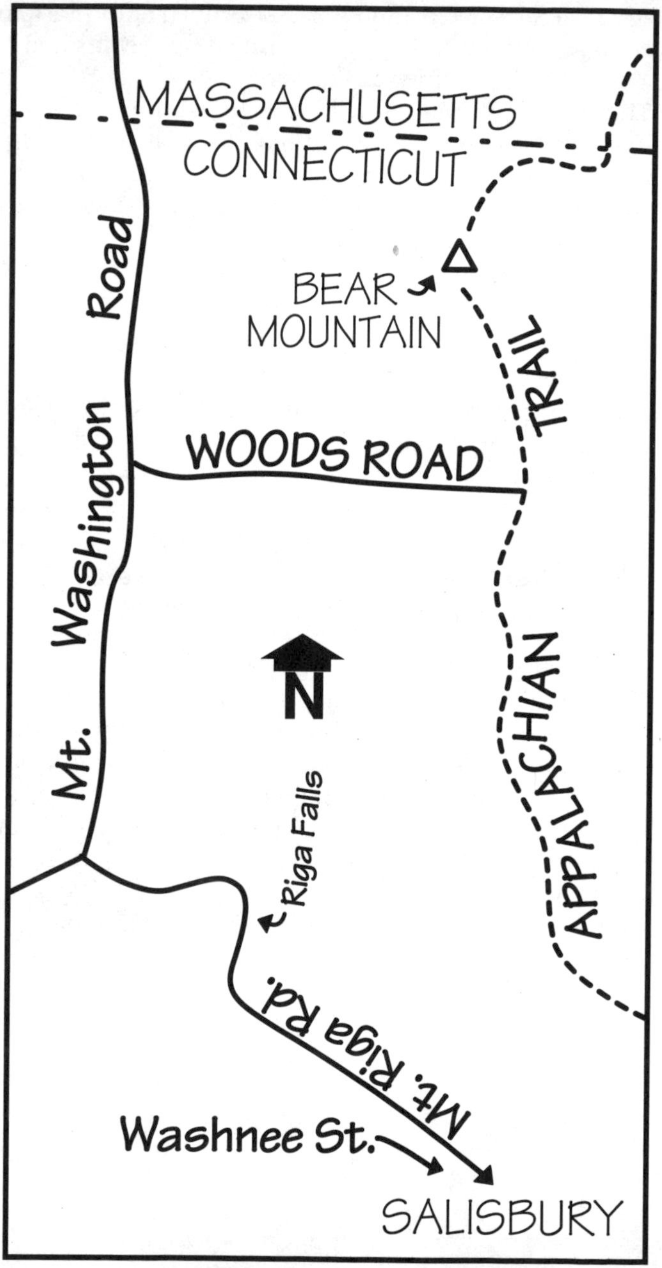

MASSACHUSETTS
CONNECTICUT
BEAR MOUNTAIN
Mt. Washington Road
TRAIL
WOODS ROAD
APPALACHIAN
N
Riga Falls
Mt. Riga Rd.
Washnee St.
SALISBURY

Bear Mountain

There is a universal allure about things that have the state or reputation of being the longest, widest, highest, or any other superlative quality. The highest point in any area seems to have special appeal for the hiker. The highest mountain peak in the world, Mount Everest, has little to offer its conquerors after they suffer the extreme hardships to reach its top, other than the satisfaction of having reached the heights. A simple explanation of this compulsive urge to climb even the smallest hill was given by George Leigh Mallory, who, when asked why he wanted to climb Mount Everest, said, "Because it is there."

Bear Mountain, because it is there and perhaps because it is the highest peak in Connecticut, attracts hundreds of hikers to its crest, which is 2,315 feet above sea level. It is the highest mountain peak entirely within the bounds of the state, but, oddly enough, it is not the highest point in the state. Connecticut's highest elevation of 2,380 feet is on the Connecticut–Massachusetts boundary line as it passes over the south shoulder of Mount Frissel, the peak of which is in Massachusetts.

Bear Mountain is in the township of Salisbury and may be reached by numerous trails, the most important of which is the Appalachian Trail. Most of these approaches are long and arduous; one of the shortest and easiest, about 1.5 miles to the crest, is via an old woods road from Mount Washington Road.

To reach the starting point of this walk, follow the most convenient route to Salisbury's town hall, which is at the corner of Route 44 and Washnee Street. From this junction, turn west onto Washnee Street and follow it .6 mile to Mount Riga Road, on the left.

Mount Riga Road is a gravel road and in places only wide enough for one car; when confronted with oncoming traffic, one car must turn out or back up to a passing place. Drive with care, as this unimproved road carries moderate traffic, and be aware that it is closed to vehicles from the first snowfall through the end of mud season, in the spring.

Follow Mount Riga Road from Washnee Street 2.8 miles to a junction with Mount Washington Road to the right. Turn sharply to the right, north, and continue 3 miles to an old woods road on the right, east. Here a white sign says HIKING TRAIL.

Park your car, being careful not to block the woods road or main road. On foot go east on the woods road, which is not blazed but is well defined. Keep on the woods road to the junction with the white-blazed Appalachian Trail at approximately 1 mile from Mount Washington Road.

Turn left, north, onto the Appalachian Trail and follow it as it ascends gradually but constantly up Bear Mountain's south face. The terrain is rocky and rough but not precipitous. The top of the mountain is covered with blueberry bushes and studded with trees misshapened and tortured by severe weather and winds.

Bear Mountain's crest is surmounted with a flat-topped pyramid-like stone monument about 10 feet high and 10 feet square at the base.

After exploring the mountain top, and lunching and resting, return down the white-blazed trail to the unblazed woods road, turning right (west), back to your starting point and car.

21

Leatherman Cave

The bankruptcy of a small leather business in France resulted in a broken betrothal and an historical legend in Connccticut, a legend that has evoked wonder and astonishment in all who have heard the anecdotes about the Old Leatherman.

Although he roamed back and forth across Connecticut for twenty-seven years, very little is known about him. Only near the close of his life were bits of his story learned. His name was Jules Bourglay; he was born near Lyons, France. He worked for his prospective father-in-law, who owned a prosperous leather business. The young man ruined the business by miscalculating the market and was then jilted by his sweetheart. These losses affected him mentally, and he became an eccentric wanderer. He left France and came to America.

The Old Leatherman was first reported in Connecticut in 1862. Thereafter he roamed the state in an oval-like circuit between the Connecticut and Hudson rivers. It is claimed that he made the trip winter and summer, arriving at the same places every thirty-four days.

He wore leather clothing from head to toe. His hat, coat, vest, trousers, and shoes were made of small pieces of hide crudely laced together. It is estimated that his attire weighed more than sixty pounds, not including two large leather bags in which he carried all his other possessions. One anecdote states that he

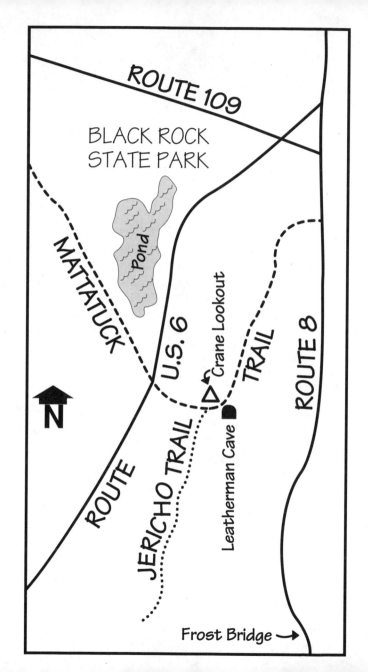

wore these things as a penance and a constant reminder of his misfortunes.

He begged food by gestures, never speaking but expressing thanks for food and tobacco with grunts. His overnight stopping place was in one of many caves along his route. He could not be persuaded to sleep in a house or barn. All his sleeping, even his last, was in a cave. He was found dead near Ossining, New York, in a cave.

If all the caves in which the Leatherman is reported to have slept had a sign "Leatherman Slept Here," these surely would outnumber Washington's sleeping places in Connecticut.

One of the numerous Leatherman caves in the state is located on the Mattatuck Trail in a segment of state forest in Watertown. To reach this cave, follow road map routes to the intersection of Route 109 with Route U.S. 6 in the town of Thomaston. Drive southwest on Route U.S. 6 for 1 mile, passing Black Rock State Park at .5 mile, to the Mattatuck Trail crossing, indicated by an oval blue-and-white trail sign and by blue-blazed trees.

Park your car and follow the blazed trail in an easterly direction over a 650-foot-high overlook with fine views. After descending from this lookout, the ascent to the top of Crane Lookout begins. The crest is reached at .9 mile from your car. Crane Lookout presents magnificent views in every direction.

At the base of Crane Lookout, south side, is Leatherman Cave, a most unusual and interesting geological formation, which is also known as Rock House. The Mattatuck Trail passes right through the cave and junctures with the Jericho Trail, a side trail leading south to Frost Bridge.

You may wish to explore the Jericho or Mattatuck trails a short distance in this area before returning to your car. (For a hike in nearby Black Rock State Park, see Walk 22.)

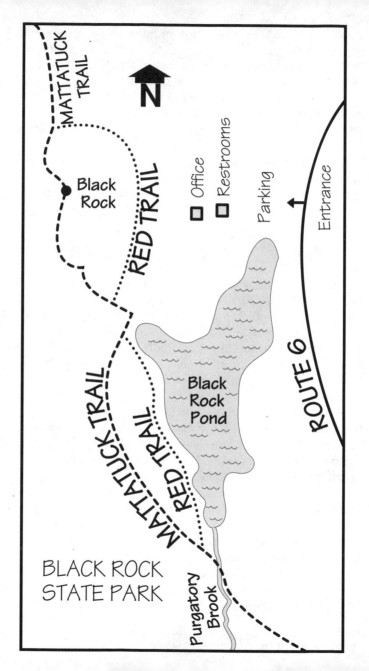

22

Black Rock

"America probably would survive without a space program. It will never survive without a conservation program." So stated Dr. Matthew Brennan, a director of the Pinchot Institute for Conservation Studies, in an address to a group of Connecticut conservationists.

Dr. Brennan said, "Every public school in America should have a green open space adjacent to it as an outdoor classroom in which boys and girls can study living nature.

"Children now learn bird songs from films. . . . They read about nature in books and see pictures of the outdoors on television, but they seldom go outdoors to learn about nature. Indoors they sing, 'I love thy rocks and rills,' but they don't know what a rill is; they have never seen one."

Dr. Brennan claimed, ". . . as far as people's understanding of the environment in which they live and depend, education has been a total failure. The serious crises of water, air, and land pollution . . . underlines this failure."

Fortunately, Connecticut conservationists have been aware of these needs for many years, not only the need to inform and educate the public but also the need to provide open space where adults as well as children may come closer to nature.

Unfortunately, there is not a green open space adjacent to every public school in Connecticut. We are, however, richly en-

dowed with state parks, state forests, nature centers, and the Connecticut Blue Trail System, all within reach of every person in the state. An important part of this nature complex is Black Rock State Park in Watertown, which has every element of an ideal nature preserve. In the rolling hills of the state's western highlands, it includes a stretch of the Mattatuck Trail as well as Black Rock Pond, Purgatory Brook, and steep ledges covered with pine, hemlock, and oak. The park was given to the people of Connecticut more than fifty years ago through the efforts of a far-sighted citizens' conservation group.

The park is located 2 miles west of Thomaston on Route 6. It has adequate parking, and restrooms are available April through October.

It is said that an early user of what are now park trails was King Philip, an Indian chief who pursued Colonial farmers in an attempt to discourage settlement. The stone points and implements of Connecticut's first residents are still found in the park.

As the Mattatuck Trail passes through the park, it skirts the shore of Black Rock Pond and ascends to Black Rock itself, a high spot providing a wonderful view of the Naugatuck Valley. The distance from the pond to the rock is less than a mile. You may retrace your steps to your starting point or continue ahead, turning right onto a red-marked trail to make a somewhat longer loop back. Alternatively, you may continue northward on the blue-blazed Mattatuck Trail to Black Rock Lake. You may also follow the Mattatuck Trail south from the park. In both its southern and northern directions, this trail goes into the Mattatuck State Forest.

23

Gillette Castle

On the east bank of the Connecticut River is a chain of hills called the Seven Sisters. The most southerly of these, the Seventh Sister, rises in the townships of Lyme and East Haddam. It straddles the Middlesex–New London county line, and from its crest one looks down upon the Chester–Hadlyme ferry slip to the south.

Atop this outstanding hill, William Hooker Gillette, famed for his stage portrayal of Sherlock Holmes, built (1914–1919) a twenty-four room, sprawling, towering medieval-like castle of fieldstone. It was Gillette's semi-retirement home until his death in 1937.

The castle and grounds were purchased by the state in 1943 to become Gillette Castle State Park, which now has 184 acres. It attracts thousands of visitors, who are permitted to enter the castle and inspect the interior and furnishings, which are approximately as used and left by Mr. Gillette. Some visitors are impressed by the interior decorations of a past era. Some are impressed or depressed by the exterior architectural style, and perhaps a few fall into the category stated in Mr. Gillette's will as, ". . . a blithering saphead who has no conception of where he is or with what surrounded."

There is an admission fee to enter the castle, which is open daily from Memorial Day to Columbus Day and weekends only

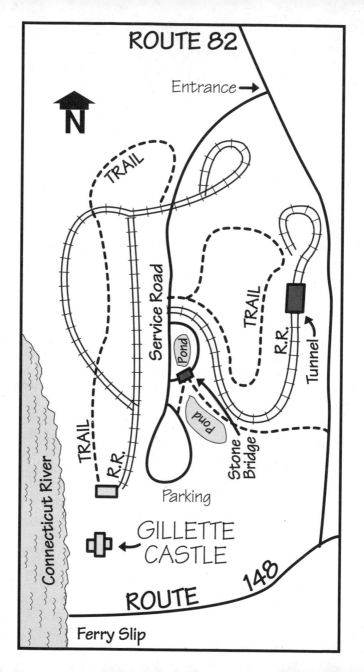

from Columbus Day until the Christmas season. The rest of the park is open all year for the pleasure of those who delight in natural things and open space. There are several woodland trails and also walking paths on former railroad beds (along which Mr. Gillette took his guests for rides in his miniature steam train). Volunteers are steadily restoring the old railroad beds and bridges for today's hikers and strollers.

To reach the entrance to Gillette Castle State Park, drive or take the Chester–Hadlyme ferry to the ferry slip on Route 148, on the east bank of the Connecticut River. From the ferry slip follow Route 148 northeast about .2 mile to a road junction. Leave Route 148 here, turning left on the road leading to the park, and follow signs to the park entrance, about .7 mile. Enter the park and follow service roads to the main parking lot. Park your car, then obtain from the ranger or the attendant a free copy of a map of the grounds, buildings, trails, and railroad right-of-way.

From year to year as we revisit forest areas, it may appear at first glance that nothing has changed. The forest seems to have a calm stability, a harmony, a feeling of something eternal that will never change. Yet there is constant change. The forest floor is covered with the litter and debris of fallen plant and animal life which is constantly under attack by such organisms as earthworms, springtails, fungi, and bacteria, and these decomposers in turn are preyed upon by larger and larger forms of life.

Every living thing develops from elements that once were a part of other living things. Our own bodies are composed of second-hand materials that may have been active ad infinitum in other forms of life. Some of the atoms and cells in our own makeup may have been functioning in the body of a giant dinosaur that once sloshed around in prehistoric swamps.

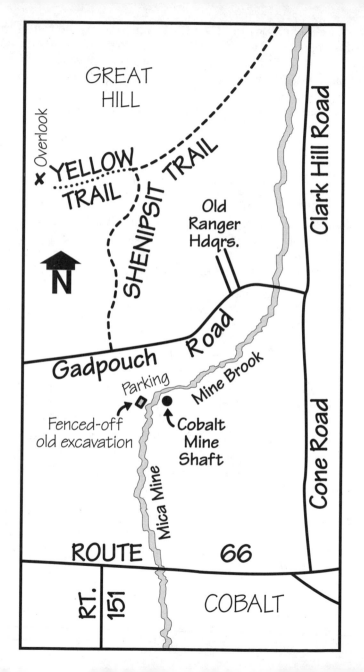

Cobalt Mine

The Cobalt Mine in the township of East Hampton should be of special interest to all who are interested in geology or history.

The mine may be reached from the junction of Route 151 with Route 66 in Cobalt. Drive east on Route 66 1.2 miles to Cone Road, on the left. Turn onto Cone Road and follow it 1 mile to Gadpouch Road; this road is also named Great Hill Road. At the junction of the three roads—Cone Road, Clark Hill Road, and Gadpouch Road—one approaches the Meshomasic State Forest. Turn left onto Gadpouch Road and follow it just under .5 mile to a fork with a dirt road on the right.

From this fork continue on Gadpouch Road a few hundred feet to an open area on the left between the road and Mine Brook. Park your car here and walk to the fenced-off, abandoned, cobalt mine excavation. Directly across Mine Brook, on its south bank, is a former opening to one of the mine shafts. The tunnel is now almost completely choked by cave-ins.

Follow Mine Brook downstream a short distance to tumbled stone foundations, all that remain of the buildings used in the mining operation. It is reported that the mine, which was started in 1792, was never a financial success.

Cobalt was used primarily for coloring fine china, especially delftware. Cobalt is the Anglicized German word *kobold*, meaning a goblin or gnome. The German miners considered cobalt a destructive force and a demon in their mines. They named the silver-white metallic element *kobold* because they thought it worthless; and when found in combination with arsenic and sulphur, it was harmful both to their health and the valuable silver ores they were mining.

South of the state forest boundary on the brook is an abandoned mica mine. Feldspar is also found in the area. Mica, due to its high electrical resistance, is used in electrical equipment. Feldspar is used by industry in manufacturing ceramics, glazes, enamels, and binders.

Time and energy permitting, you can visit another point of interest in the immediate vicinity, Great Hill, 770 feet above sea level. The blue-blazed Shenipsit Trail leads to the crest of Great Hill. It starts several hundred feet west of the picnic ground, from the north shoulder of Great Hill Road.

Follow the blue-blazed trail as it ascends quite steeply for .4 mile to a junction with a yellow-blazed trail at the top of the ridge. The Shenipsit Trail turns north; the yellow-blazed trail leads south to the overlook on Great Hill. The junction is marked by a small cairn monument.

The view from the overlook is spectacular: On a clear day Long Island Sound is plainly visible; Great Hill Pond is over 400 feet below; the long sweep of the Connecticut River as it flows east and then south through this section of the Connecticut Valley is breathtaking.

25

Meshomasic Forest

The Meshomasic Forest is Connecticut's first state forest. It has many attractive features, the Shenipsit Trail being one of them.

The Shenipsit Trail is considered a through trail in spite of one 11-mile gap and a few stretches by road. It totals some 30 miles in length from Cobalt in the township of East Hampton to the Massachusetts state line. A spectacular feature of the trail is Great Hill, located at the trail's southern terminus.

Great Hill is literally and figuratively the high point of Meshomasic State Forest and the Shenipsit Trail. To reach this point, follow the most convenient route to the junction of Routes 66 and 151 in the Cobalt section of East Hampton. Drive east on Route 66 1.2 miles to Cone Road, on the left. Turn onto Cone Road and follow it 1 mile to the junction with Gadpouch Road and Clark Hill Road. Follow Clark Hill Road, a right fork, .7 mile to a dirt service road called Woodchopper Road. Turn left onto this road and follow it .6 mile to the Shenipsit Trail crossing, indicated by blue-blazed trees.

Park your car and follow the blazed trail south. At about 1.75 miles the main trail turns left and a yellow-blazed trail leads several hundred feet to the bald cap of Great Hill. This is the ideal spot to rest and lunch while taking in the exceptional views of Great Hill Pond directly below and the broad sweep of the Connecticut River cradled by the towering hills. Retracing your

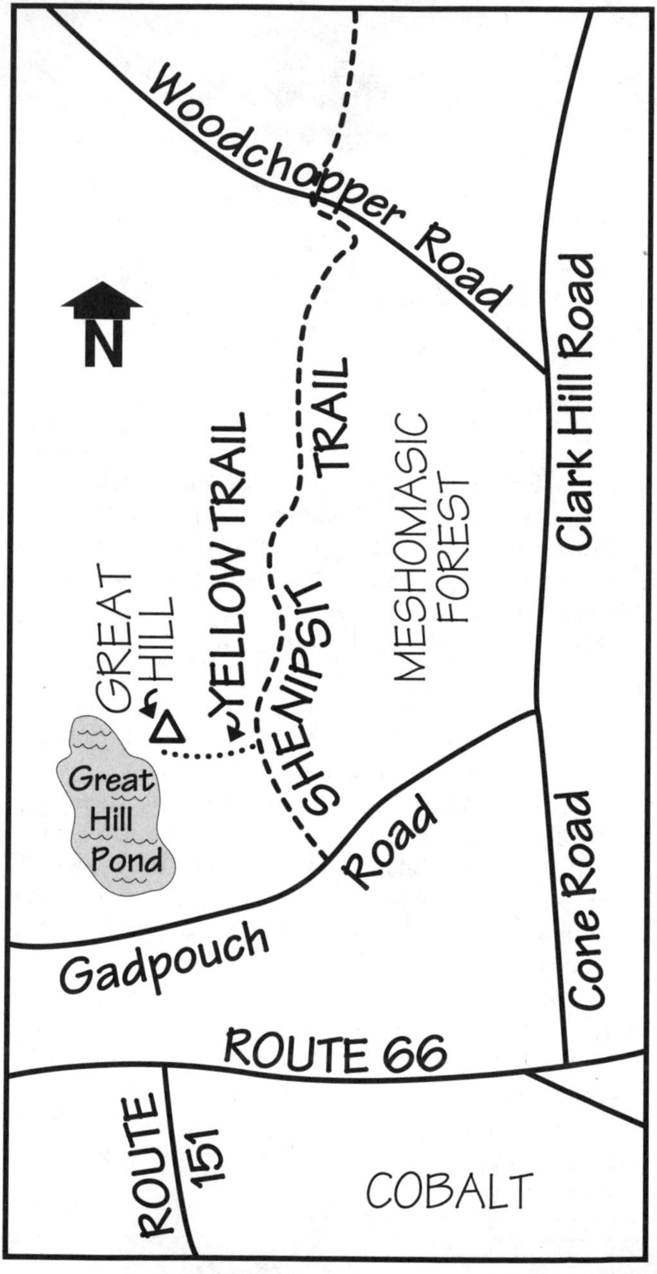

N

Woodchopper Road

Clark Hill Road

YELLOW TRAIL

SHENIPSIT TRAIL

MESHOMASIC FOREST

GREAT HILL

Great Hill Pond

Road

Cone Road

Gadpouch

ROUTE 66

ROUTE 151

COBALT

steps from Gadpouch to your parked car, the round-trip is about 4 miles.

Shortly after the first fall frost, the moment of truth arrives for all male bees, drones, in all honeybee colonies. Drones are incapable of caring for the young, making wax, or gathering nectar or pollen. Their sole purpose for being is to mate with a princess, who then becomes a queen. Only one of several thousand drones will have this privilege. The drones perform no other service for the colony.

During the height of the harvest, sterile female workers will tolerate the hundreds of drones usually present in most hives. The workers seem to have great affection for their handsome, bumbling brothers. A drone will stop a sister carrying food, confront her head-on, and extend his tongue; the nurse bee will then give him a droplet of food.

After the first killing frost, all affection is forgotten. Only those members of the colony who can be of use during the long winter months are allowed to remain in the hive. The now useless, luckless drones must go.

Every last drone is dragged from the recesses of the hive and forced outside, away from the warmth and food. It takes several sisters to handle their stronger, bulkier brothers, who naturally persist in getting back into the heart of the family.

Should he be too persistent, the sisters resort to a final indignity. They nip off his wings, and one of them drags the wingless drone up the outside of the hive. Having gained sufficient altitude, she casts off with her heavy load and glides away as far as possible, then drops the victim. The drone, unable to fly or crawl back home, dies.

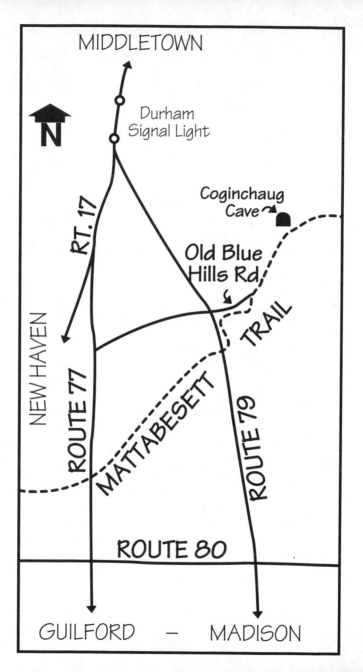

26

Coginchaug Cave

A most fascinating rock cliff called Coginchaug Cave will interest and intrigue you.

Coginchaug Cave is located in the town of Durham on a section of the Mattabesett Trail. Follow Connecticut road map routes to Durham Center. Start from the signal light at the junction of Routes 17 and 79, and drive south on Route 79 .8 mile to Old Blue Hills Road. Turn left (east) and follow blue blazes on poles and trees to the end of the surfaced road, .3 mile from Route 79.

Park your car off the turnaround at the end of the blacktop. Follow the marked path up a fair grade, at the top of which a trail turns right, leading in an easterly direction. Follow its winding course between ledges and over ridges, crossing brooks and swampy areas on convenient stepping stones. The cave is .8 mile from the parking area. Before reaching the cave, you will be confronted with a stiff climb to a high ridge, under which Coginchaug Cave lies. Leave the ridge and descend a steep slope down the face of the ledge. This part of the trail is a little tricky, and care should be taken. Within a few yards the footing eases as the path widens and leads into the cave from the south.

Coginchaug Cave is quite impressive. It is a large shelter cave 30 feet high, 20 feet deep, and extends more than 50 feet along the base of the cliff. It has been reported that some Indian artifacts, arrowheads, and tools have been found here.

After spending as much time as you desire in the area, return to your car by retracing the trail. The walk may easily be done in an hour. Should you wish to spend more time at the cave or along the trail, take a lunch and make a day of it. This walk is planned for an easy family outing. Those who wish to extend themselves a little may do so by following the blue blazes down from the cave, crossing the brook in the valley. Ascend the winding trail through heavy hemlock growth and over huge bald rocks to the top of Blue Hill Lookout. This is a sheer cliff with a deep valley below and a rewarding view over woodlands, fields, meadows, and high ridges to the west. Continue to follow the blazed trail until you feel you've had enough. Remember that at this point you have walked only halfway; don't overdo. Return along the trail to your car, and then return home both tired and refreshed from an inspiring change of pace.

Pistapaug Mountain

More than one hundred years ago, Ralph Waldo Emerson wrote, "At the gates of the forest the surprised man of the world is forced to leave his city estimates of great and small, wise and foolish. . . . In the woods we return to reason and faith."

Today, due to the forethought and effort of many people, we in our state enjoy a rich heritage of forest and natural lands in which we may roam and return to reason and faith.

One of the many beautiful spots along Connecticut's Blue Trail System is Pistapaug Mountain and Pond. The mountain is located on the Mattabesett Trail in the town of Durham, west of Route 17.

The trail begins about 3 miles south of the intersection of Routes 17 and 77 and about a mile north of the North Branford/Durham town line.

Park safely off Route 17 and follow blazed trees on the west side of the road. Near the guardrail of a small highway bridge, the trail enters the woods, crosses a small brook, then follows north along the brook for about 100 yards. After turning left, it follows along an old woods road a short distance before turning north and then up to the ridge of Pistapaug Mountain. The top of the mountain is about 1 mile from the parking area. Follow the marked trail to openings in the heavy growth of hemlock.

From the edge of these hemlock-covered bluffs, elevation 700

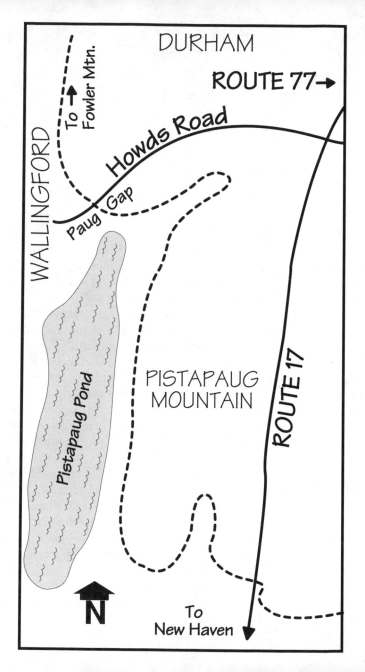

feet, is to be had the finest view of Pistapaug Pond, hundreds of feet below. A grand view to the west and south of these openings brings into sight a far-flung panorama of gently rolling farmland—irregularly shaped fields dotted with white farmhouses, red barns, and silos.

Having satiated your eyes and senses, you may wish to go on. The trail continues down a steep woods road to Paug Gap, 1.9 miles from your starting point. The trail crosses Howds Road and ascends Fowler Mountain, but it would be advisable to leave this for another day. Retrace your steps along the trail to the top of Pistapaug Mountain and then down to your car.

After a view, your trip down the west side of the mountain may prove anticlimactic; yet the true hiker may very well press on the additional 2 miles just to see what's on the other side.

These short walks will be most enjoyable if there is no rush to reach this or that objective. Take your time and appreciate the trail as you traverse it. Observe the growth on the trail and alongside it; learn to identify the trees and plants, and you will double your appreciation of these trails.

The landscape you view belongs to you whether you own the land or not. Emerson expressed this when he said, "The charming landscape which I saw this morning is indubitably made up of some twenty or thirty farms; Miller owns this field, Locke that, and Manning the woodland beyond. But none of these own the landscape. There is a property in the horizon which no man owns but he whose eyes can integrate all the parts. . . . This is the best part of these men's farms, yet to this their warranty-deeds give no title."

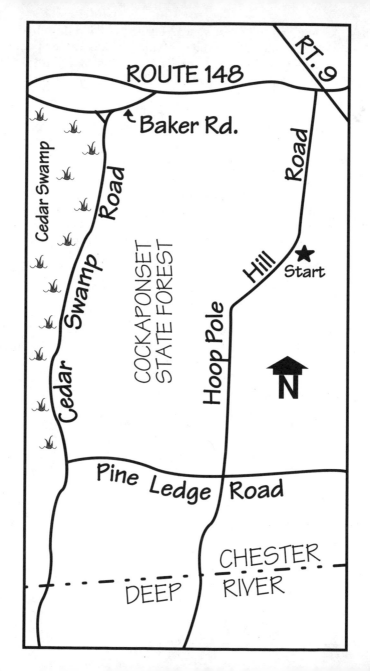

28

Hoop Pole Hill

The Connecticut state forests are maintained chiefly as recreational outlets and for timber production. Timbering operations seldom interfere with the use of the forests by the public. The value of the timber crops may easily be tallied, but the pleasure derived by the public in the use of our forests can never be appraised, as the fringe benefits are incalculable.

The Cockaponset State Forest has been divided, for management purposes, into four major blocks: Turkey Hill, Winthrop, Cedar Swamp, and Killingworth. This Hoop Pole Hill walk is in the Cedar Swamp block and follows woods and main roads to complete a loop of approximately 4 miles.

Follow Route 9 north or south to Exit 6 and the interchange with Route 148 in Chester. Hoop Pole Hill Road is at the southwest corner of the intersection. Follow Hoop Pole Hill Road south .8 mile to the end of the improved road. Park your car so as not to block the highway, private drive, or woods service roads.

Continue afoot southwest on Hoop Pole Hill Road to the intersection with Pine Ledge Road. Turn right onto Pine Ledge Road (approximately 1 mile from Route 148 and .2 mile from where the pavement ends on Hoop Pole) and follow it west to the junction with Cedar Swamp Road. Turn right, north, onto Cedar Swamp Road and follow it to surfaced Baker Road. From your parked car to this point is about 2.5 miles, or 5 miles round-trip. The trail is not blazed but follows well-defined woods roads. You may retrace your steps from Baker Road or any other previous point along the way.

To complete the 4-mile loop turn right, east, onto Baker Road, and follow it to the junction with Route 148. Then continue east on the highway to Route 9 and Hoop Pole Hill Road, a distance of .2 mile. Turn south onto Hoop Pole Hill Road and follow it .8 of a mile to your parked car.

The Hoopole Hill walk has little to offer in overlooks, ledges, ponds, or anything extraordinary. It is just an easy, pleasant walk that nonetheless has much to give to those who take time to look, see, and wonder.

It requires patience to discover and observe the minute adventures and misadventures taking place all around us, especially in natural areas such as are to be found in a state forest.

To sit quietly for long periods to observe the engineering skill of a common spider weaving her web can be as satisfying as a costly safari to hunt more glamorous game. To watch a spider in her completed web, waiting expectantly for a juicy morsel to become ensnared in her trap, can be more interesting and entertaining than the general run of television offerings.

Mythology has given the spider her scientific name, *arachnid*. Arachne, a skilled Lydian girl, immodestly challenged Athene, goddess of wisdom and patroness of the womanly art of weaving, to a contest at the loom. They began weaving; Athene depicted the power and glory of the gods, while Arachne set forth their weaknesses. Athene destroyed Arachne's magnificent tapestry as a penalty for the girl's insolence. Arachne attempted to hang herself, but Athene foiled the attempt and changed Arachne into a spider, condemned to dangle and spin forever.

29

Hurd Park

The very first state park site on the Connecticut River was Hurd Park, in the township of East Hampton. Today, its 884 acres are ideal for hiking and picnicking, and it has many secluded spots where those seeking solitude may find it.

Hurd Brook and the Connecticut River are among this park's many attractions. There are several hiking trails, including the Split Rock Trail. These trails lead through heavily wooded areas; some ascend to high ground where excellent views present themselves.

Hurd Park is on the east side of the Connecticut River. The main entrance to the park may be reached from the junction of Hurd Park Road with Route 151. An overhead traffic light 2.5 miles south of Route 66, or 3 miles north of Route 196 on Route 151, marks the junction. From this junction turn south onto Hurd Park Road and follow it .6 mile to the gateway entrance to the park. Follow the surfaced service road to a turnaround; park your car after selecting the area you wish to explore. The trails are marked and should prove easy to follow. The Split Rock Trail leads to a large fissure in a ledge and an excellent view of the Connecticut River and the river valley. What is known as the Power Line Trail follows an access road to the power lines and continues to the meadows next to the river, in adjoining George D. Seymour State Park, in the township of Haddam, to the south.

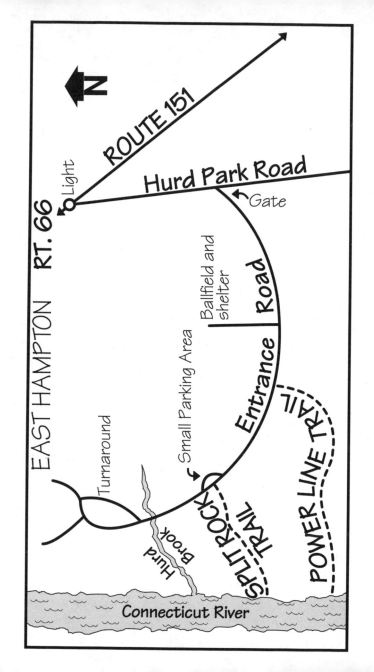

It has been said that any plant man cannot use is classified as a weed. The common milkweed, whose botanical name is *asclepias syriaca,* is also known as "Judas flower" and "pinchtrap." It has many virtues, but beekeepers believe it has an equal number of faults.

Milkweed has a reputation for secreting nectar very rapidly—a nectar that produces quantities of excellent honey. However, it is more celebrated for its queer, unique method of having its life-perpetuating pollen grains distributed from flower to flower by entrapment of the honeybee.

Like Judas, the perfidious milkweed betrays its most faithful friend and benefactor, the honeybee, without whose pollinating services the milkweed might become extinct.

The offering of a plentiful supply of rich nectar induces the foraging honeybee to land on the milkweed flower, the petals of which are so slippery she is unable to gain a secure footing. One or both hind legs may slide into the heart of the flower, where they become entangled with the twin-winged pollen balls. Old and enfeebled bees cannot free themselves from these appendages and lose their lives. The healthy, stronger bees are able to pull the winged pollen mass free from the blossom and carry it, like a prisoner's ball and chain, to the next flower, where cross-fertilization takes place and the bee is able to leave a part of the hindering hobble behind.

Why did the milkweed family find it necessary to evolve this remarkable device? It is found in no other family of plants in the world. Was it the only way it could accomplish pollination? Or is it because nature is so profligate with expendable bees?

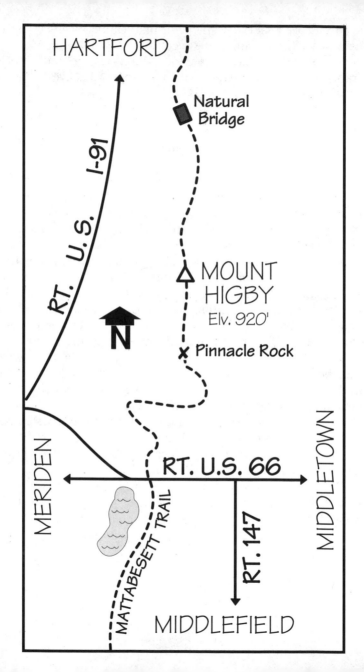

30

Mount Higby

One of the most popular short walks on Connecticut's trail system is to Mount Higby. The view from its crest extends almost 360 degrees from Mount Tom, Massachusetts, to Long Island Sound at New Haven. A portion of the trail runs near the edge of the cliff, from which are presented some breathtaking views. Mount Higby is the second highest point in Middlesex County. It may be reached easily from any part of the state.

The mountain is located partly in the towns of Middlefield and Middletown, north of U.S. Route 66, close to the eastern boundary of Meriden. To reach the point where the Mattabesett Trail ascends the mountain, follow Connecticut road maps to the junction of Routes U.S. 66 and 147. Starting at this junction, proceed west on U.S. 66 toward Meriden. At .3 mile, Mattabesett crosses the highway. Continue to the next highway sign (MERIDEN, NEXT 8 EXITS), just before Route 66 becomes Route I–691. There, on the north side of the highway, an unmarked but visible trail leads to the main trail at .1 mile. Park your car off the traveled portion of the highway and ascend in a northerly direction. (Or you may park the car behind Guida's Dairy Bar, at the intersection of Routes 66 and 147, and take the access trail—marked with purple dots—to the main trails.)

The trail swings west from Route U.S. 66 to an old woods road; at about .4 mile the trail turns right (north), ascending a steep ridge via several switchbacks. Pinnacle Rock atop Mount Higby is 1 mile from Route 66. From Pinnacle Rock one has the best viewpoint of the surrounding countryside: Hartford and Mount Tom to the north, Meriden toward the west, and a far-reaching view to the south, including Mount Beseck, with Black Pond at its base.

The bare rock formation here clearly shows how this type of basalt came to be called traprock. The word "trap" is a modification of the Swedish word *trappa,* which means stair. The rock was so named from its general appearance as a set of steps. As you go up and down these stones, notice how they resemble a gigantic staircase.

One hundred feet north of the Pinnacle is a large, bare area of basalt, quite flat, on the surface of which glacial grooves are easily distinguishable. From this point the trail descends to Preston Notch. In colonial days, the old stagecoach road passed through this notch between Middletown and Meriden.

Should you wish to extend your walk, you may continue to the northern part of Mount Higby, a stiff climb to its 892-foot elevation. Here is an interesting rock formation called the Natural Bridge. It is indicated by the abbreviation N.B. on a small marker.

When retracing your steps down the trail, keep the blue blazes in sight, as there are a few well-worn, unblazed side paths that could lead you astray. In descending, take time to observe the variety of trees with wildflowers along the path. A pocket tree and/or flower guide may prove of value in helping you identify trees and flowers.

Then again you may prefer to go along with Walt Whitman when he said, "You must not know too much, or be too precise or scientific about birds and trees and flowers, et cetera; a certain free margin, and even vagueness—perhaps ignorance, credulity—helps your enjoyment of these things."

31

Chatfield Trail

A fine woodland walk can be enjoyed on the Chatfield Trail in Killingworth. The trail begins on a woods road on the south side of Route 80, 1.35 miles west of Route 81 and 2.55 miles east of Route 79, 1 mile west of an exit from Chatfield Hollow State Park across the road. It is about 4.3 miles long. You may walk the entire trail or turn back at any point. At a little under 1.5 miles into the walk, an alternate trail makes a half-mile loop. You can take the loop and return to the main trail to make a round-trip of about 4 miles. Or you can avoid the trail altogether and stay on the woods road, which continues to Champlin Road.

At .5 mile the trail leaves the woods road and travels over ledges. At about .75 mile it passes under a large ledge.

The trail then passes a pine forest, a bog, and more large ledges before intersecting with the above-mentioned alternate trail on the right. Taking the alternate trail, you pass a swamp and a small falls, cross a brook, and reach Champlin Road, a dirt road that will return you to the main trail about 2 miles from where you started.

Continuing on the main trail, you follow along high ledges, then descend to an old road at 2 miles. This road turns left to enter Champlin Road, where the alternate trail comes back. The main trail arrives at a large rock overhang a bit before the 3-mile mark, crosses a small brook at 3.5 miles, and comes to Chatfield

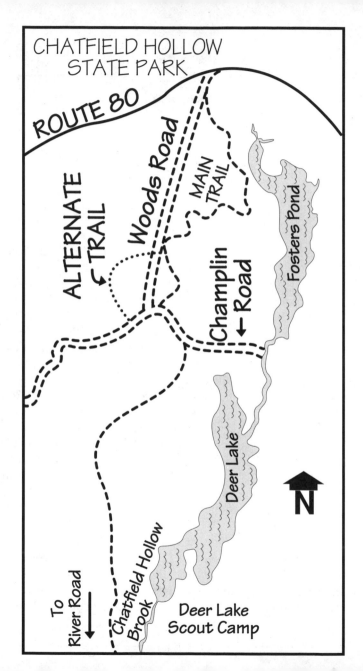

Hollow Brook at just under 4 miles. It follows the brook to reach River Road at 4.3 miles.

All woods trails, depending upon the amount of moisture, are usually decorated with colorful fungi. You will be fascinated by the normal display of toadstools or mushrooms, surprised by their number, shapes, and vivid coloring. The colors range from pure white to absolute black and a gamut of shades of tan, yellow, red, green, blue, and purple.

There is no visible difference between a toadstool and a mushroom. Both names mean the same thing: a fungus that propagates from a spore instead of a seed, having a common root system of fine threads and subsisting upon dead and living organic matter. One of its chief characteristics is the absence of chlorophyll.

Many of the more than 3,000 varieties of wild mushrooms growing in the western hemisphere are to be found along the blue-blazed trails of Connecticut. Some of the common species are puffball; beefsteak; olavaria, a member of the coral fungus group; jack o'lantern, the underside of which glows at night; and sulphur or chicken, which when fried is a gourmet's delight but is unpopular with conservationists because it often kills the tree on which it grows.

The common mushroom sold in the markets is the meadow mushroom. Oddly enough its closest look-alike is the most deadly of all known poisonous mushrooms, the destroying angel or fly amanita.

There are many rules and hints about how to detect the poisonous from the edible mushrooms, but there are also too many exceptions. So until you become an expert in fungiology, continue to have fun by admiring rather than devouring these pop-ups of nature.

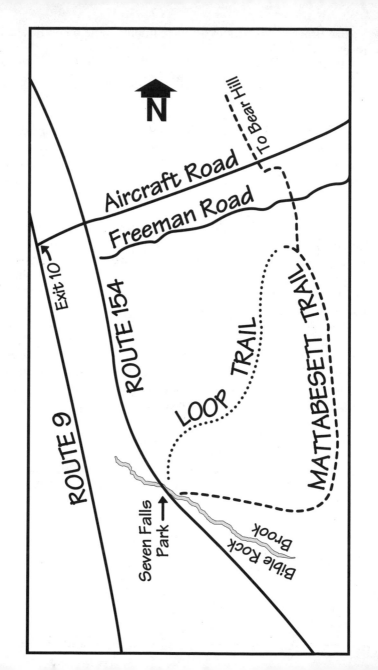

Seven Falls

Unlike most other blue-blazed through trails in Connecticut that have been curtailed and disrupted by the advance of civilization, the Mattabesett Trail is, gratifyingly, being extended and supplemented.

The Seven Falls segment of the Mattabesett lies between Route 154 and Aircraft Road. This section of the trail is about 1.7 miles long and boasts an excellent roadside park and picnic area at its Route 154 terminus in Haddam.

This part of the Mattabesett Trail may be reached either from Aircraft Road in Middletown or Seven Falls Park on Route 154 in Haddam. The easier approach to describe is from Aircraft Road.

Follow the most convenient route to Exit 10 of Route 9, in Middletown. Exit from Route 9 to Route 154 and the Aircraft Road intersection. From the intersection follow Aircraft Road cast .8 mile to a blue-blazed trail crossing.

Park your car well off the traveled portion of highway, which is quite busy during certain periods of the day. Follow the main trail southwest over interesting and rugged terrain, or pick up the loop trail that begins just beyond Freeman Road (bear right). These trails have no unusual elevations or overlooks, but the main trail follows Bible Rock Brook, with its fascinating falls and pools, in the area of Seven Falls Park and has a very special appeal.

You may stop to rest and lunch at any suitable spot along

the trail, but the ideal place to picnic is at the roadside park, where there are tables, benches, fireplaces, and toilet facilities. If time is not a factor, you may explore and enjoy the brook and its many facets for hours before returning to your car.

We can't all explore outer space, nor does everyone have a desire to do so. It is not even necessary to visit distant places on earth to see and experience extraordinary sights. One can find exciting adventure, surprising worlds, and apparent miracles right underfoot.

The universally famous "Homer of Insects," Jean Henri Fabre, spent a lifetime studying, discovering, and recording the activities of the myriad insect worlds within the confines of his small garden. Extreme poverty prevented Fabre from going places he dreamed about as a boy. Yet his own backyard gave him as much excitement, adventure, pleasure, and perhaps greater fame than he would have gained had his boyhood dreams of travel been realized.

Just one step from our own doorstep, or a few steps farther to the blue-blazed trails of Connecticut, are to be found natural miracles to enthrall the most blasé. The only requirement is that one go afoot slowly, with curiosity and a willingness to patiently watch and wonder. At first one must learn the art of seeing, not just looking.

A few of the most common insects that are easily observed are spiders, ants, wasps, bumblebees, ladybugs, and dragon-flies; each has a story to tell. The spider constructing her expertly engineered web; the carpenter ants herding and milking their domesticated cows, the aphids; and the tiny spittlebug hiding safely in her white bubbly foam nest in the grass are all fair game to the observant eye.

33

Bear Hill

The northern half of the Bear Hill section of the Mattabesett Trail has been bushcd and blazed.

This is a pleasant section of the eastern end of the Mattabesett Trail in Middletown. Future plans are to continue the Bear Hill segment east to the Connecticut River.

One need not wait for the completion of these plans to enjoy a walk over Bear Hill, the Summit, or the Chinese Wall, all of which are now part of the Mattabesett Trail. To reach this section of the trail, follow the most convenient route to Route 154, Saybrook Road, in Middletown.

Approaching from the north, drive to the junction of Routes 155 and 154. From the junction follow Route 154 south .2 mile to Brooks Road; turn east onto Brooks Road and follow .8 mile to the blue-blazed trail.

Approaching from the south from the intersection of Aircraft Road and Route 154, follow Route 154 north 1.1 miles to Tollgate Road. Turn northeast onto Tollgate Road and follow .5 mile to Brooks Road. Turn right onto Brooks Road and follow .6 mile to the blue-blazed trail (which is .15 mile past Bear Hill Road).

Park your car and follow the self-guiding trail south, crossing Bear Hill Road, and continue to the crest of Bear Hill. This segment of the Mattabesett Trail is made up of a main trail and several loops. The main trail is indicated by blue-blazed rectangles;

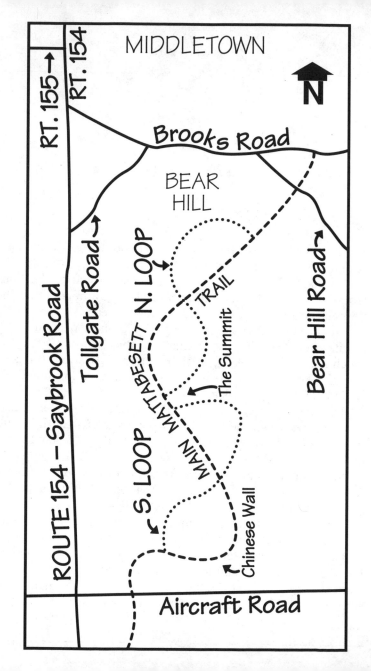

the connecting loop trails are marked with circular blue blazes. Take care; confusion is possible.

The main trail extends approximately 3.5 miles between Brooks Road and Aircraft Road.

A person's five senses are inferior to those of insects collectively. Depending on its needs, each insect has developed one or more of the five senses—vision, sound, scent, taste, or touch—to a degree superior to that of man. It is true this superiority may extend to only one sense, leaving the others in a second-rate state of development compared to man.

Since the honeybee cannot hear and her vision is limited, she has to find other means to signal and recognize her sisters directly. Bees of each species are so identical in appearance they have to use a means of positively identifying their individual family members. Their infallible method is to use a distinct odor. For this purpose, honeybees have a highly developed scent gland and antennae with a miraculous power to broadcast and detect odors.

The honeybee's scent gland is located on top of her abdomen, near the tail. When in use, the body segments separate to expose the gland. The scent is spread by vigorous wing fanning. In this manner, bees broadcast their presence to other members of the colony from hive or flower.

This broadcasting would be ineffective without a proper receiving device, the bee's antennae. These thread-like, jointed organs are covered with microscopic plates that are so sensitive a bee can pick up odor-waves from great distances.

The honeybee perfected her "smell radar" millions of years ago and has been using it successfully ever since.

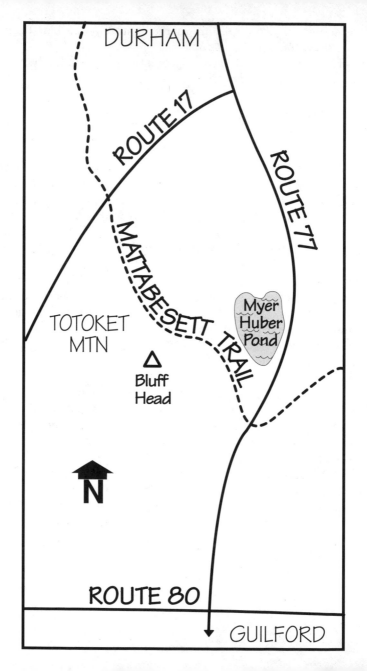

34

Bluff Head

Bluff Head is on the Mattabesett Trail in the town of Guilford. Its base is easily reached by car. The ascent afoot presents a heady and breath-taking climb and view.

Follow road map routes either to the junction of Routes 17 and 77 in Durham or to the intersection of Routes 77 and 80 in Guilford, whichever is nearer. The Mattabesett Trail leading to Bluff Head crosses Route 77 about halfway between Route 17 (Durham) and Route 80 (Guilford). The distance is about 4.3 miles from Route 80 and 4 miles from Route 17.

Turn west off Route 77 onto a dirt road at blue-blazed poles and trees. Park your car off the road near the beginning of the foot trail.

The blue-blazed trail is sharply inclined from the very start and presents a stiff climb. In the short distance of 500 feet the trail rises 190 feet in height. Although the very beginning of the trail is unusually precipitous, it is so for only a short distance. After about 550 feet the trail incline lessens and the ascent is easier.

Be properly prepared for this walk with suitable shoes; do not try to negotiate the steep ascent with slippery leather soles. Wearing slippery footgear on the trail can be treacherous, particularly when coming down.

After the first hard climb, the trail is less steep and ascends obliquely toward the north. At the top of the first rise on the right (east), the cliff makes a sheer fall of several hundred feet to the road below.

Bluff Head is 720 feet above sea level. The views from the top edge of its cliffs are as awesome as any scene in the state. Long Island Sound far to the south, the heart-shaped Myer Huber Pond to the east and 500 feet below, the fields and distant hills to the north—all invite more than a second look.

Leaving the edge of the bluff, the trail changes course from north to west and crosses a high plateau where once stood a lookout tower for observing forest fires. Only the concrete footings remain. When the tower stood here, it was a sky-scraping landmark that could be seen for miles around.

From the lookout tower site the trail heads in a general westerly direction across Totoket Mountain and down to Route 17, 3 miles from Route 77.

Bluff Head is a delightful place to spend an hour or a day. Take a lunch and enjoy it while viewing the far-flung scenes from any of the interesting overlooks on the trail. Though water may be found in streams near the trail, it is advisable to carry your own "sure water" or other liquids for drinking in thermos or canteen.

When returning and descending the last few hundred feet of the trail from Bluff Head, take care; the sliding, slippery shale can cause severe spills. Always use caution in the woods and on the trail; Mother Nature may appear gentle, but she penalizes without discrimination the heedless and the thoughtless.

Back at our starting point, we may be a bit weary and tired; it is a satisfying weariness, however; and with it we realize that contentment comes from the enjoyment of simple things.

35

Hanging Hills: East Peak

The Metacomet Trail passes over the Hanging Hills of Meriden as well as over the striking traprock range running to the Massachusetts state line. The length of the trail in Connecticut is approximately 45 miles; it continues across Massachusetts to Mount Monadnock in New Hampshire.

Metacomet was the name of "King Philip," an Indian who held dominion over this area during colonial days. It is alleged that he directed the burning of Simsbury from one of the summits on this trail, which today bears his name.

One of the most interesting features of the Metacomet Trail is to be found on the section that passes over the east and west peaks of the Hanging Hills. Both peaks are in Meriden's Hubbard Park, and both can be reached by car when the park roads are open to vehicles (April 1–October 31, 10:00 A.M. to 5:00 P.M.). West Peak, with an elevation of 1,024 feet, offers one of the finest views in Connecticut. East Peak is not quite as high, but it has a stone observation tower, Castle Craig, that offers unobstructed views of distant horizons.

After viewing the far-flung landscape from both peaks, you may wish to walk the blue-blazed trail leading down from East Peak. This section of the trail skirts the very brink of the cliffs on the west side of Merimere Reservoir.

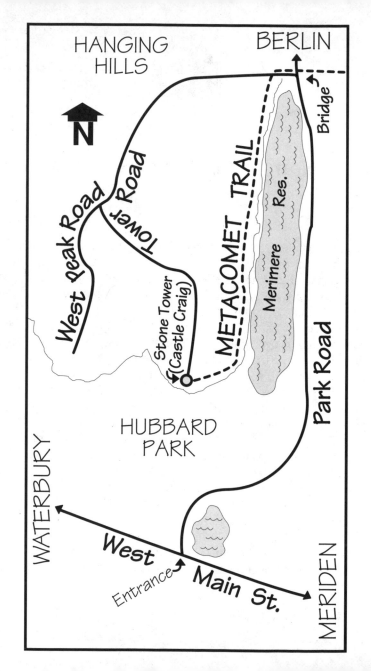

To reach the starting point for this walk, follow road map routes (Route I–691, exit 4, works well) to Hubbard Park, on West Main Street in Meriden.

From West Main turn north into the park entrance just west of Mirror Lake (small pond). Follow the park road, taking each left turn as it presents itself. Pass the entire length of Merimere Reservoir to the concrete bridge at its north end. The bridge is 1.7 miles from West Main Street. Turn left (west), cross the bridge, and follow Tower Road. The first signs of the blue trail are to be seen here on the bridge and trees on the north side of the road. (The blazed trail follows the road for .2 mile from the bridge, at which point it leaves the road and leads south along the west bank of the reservoir.) Continue to drive along Tower Road from the bridge for 1.4 miles to the first left-hand road. Turn left, easterly, and continue .5 mile to a stone tower, Castle Craig, on East Peak.

Leave your car in the parking area. East of the parking area and a short distance northeast of the tower, the trail is indicated by blue-blazed trees. Follow the trail to where it emerges on the very brink of the cliffs, which rise abruptly above Merimere Reservoir. The trail skirts the cliff's edge and gives unrivalled views of the reservoir and Mine Island, resembling a floating battleship at its southern end.

You may either make the walk by traversing as much of the trail as you wish and retracing your steps back to your parked car; or you can follow the trail to its juncture with Tower Road and return by road. It is 1.6 miles to the stone tower via the road.

Note: Both this walk and Walk 36 are in the same park.

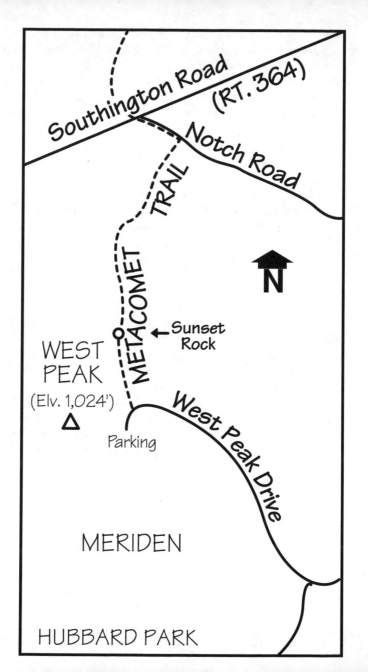

36

Hanging Hills: West Peak

Seldom does a traprock ridge present impressive views from its crest as well as from its base. But the Hanging Hills of Meriden are outstanding landmarks, dominating the scene for miles around, and the views from their peaks are among the finest in the state.

The blue-blazed Metacomet Trail has been routed along the very edge of the Hanging Hills' sheer cliffs to take advantage of the numerous overlooks. One of the most spectacular sections of the Metacomet Trail lies between West Peak and Sunset Rock, .6 mile northwest. (For a walk from the East Peak, see Walk 35.)

To reach this section, take Route I–691, Exit 4, or another convenient route to the entrance to Hubbard Park on West Main Street in Meriden. Take the park entrance just west of Mirror Lake, the park's small pond. (See map on page 104.)

When the park roads are open to vehicles (April 1–October 31, 10 A.M. to 5 P.M.), you can travel by car for part of this journey. Follow the park road on the east bank of Merimere Reservoir to the bridge. Here, go left on Tower Road; then veer right onto West Peak Drive where Tower Road goes left to Castle Craig, the stone observation tower on East Peak. You can leave your car in the parking area at West Peak (1,024 feet above sea level).

Pick up the trail near a blue-blazed pole at the northwest corner of the parking lot (close to West Peak Drive), and follow it in a general northerly direction, past a power station at the start of the trail. The main trail follows an interior course with side trails leading to outlook points. About .6 mile from West Peak, the trail reaches Sunset Rock, with its exceptional western view.

This walk should be taken at a leisurely pace, and all side trails to the left (even those right from the parking lot) should be explored, as each presents a view that is rarely matched from any other Connecticut trail.

At 3 miles from its starting point, the trail reaches Notch Road, an old woods road, leading to Southington Road, Route 364. Returning from this point, the round-trip will be 6.4 miles.

Connecticut's official state tree is the white oak. Botanists have given it the Latin name *Quercus alba*, meaning white oak, and classify it as a member of the *Fagaceae* (beech) family.

The white oak is an important timber tree, useful and valuable. Its tough, hard, close-grained, durable wood has many uses in general construction, shipbuilding, furniture making, cooperage, flooring, etc. The tree's natural range is practically all of the eastern half of the United States. The average white oak attains a height of 80 to 100 feet and a diameter of 2 to 3 feet. It is one of the easiest of oaks to identify because of its distinctive light ashy-gray bark. The full-grown leaves are bright green above and much lighter below, 5 to 9 inches long and 2 to 3 inches broad, with seven or nine deeply cut, finger-like lobes. The white oak's fruit is an acorn, which matures in one year; some oaks require two years to produce fruit. The white oak acorn grows to ¾ inch to 1 inch in length, is light brown in color, and is topped with a warty cap.

Acorns, being rich in protein and carbohydrates, sweet, and easy to chew, are prized by many animals for their food value. To the American Indian the acorn was the "staff of life."

37

High Rock

High in the Naugatuck State Forest is a popular recreation area, open to the public for picnicking and hiking. There are numerous hiking paths in this segment of the forest. Although not too well blazed, the trails are well trodden and easy to follow. The most spectacular and most popular of these walks is the one leading to the top of High Rock. From the crest, one has a fine view of the Naugatuck Valley and surrounding countryside. (To explore another lovely spot in this forest, Spruce Brook Ravine, see Walk 37.)

High Rock is in the township of Beacon Falls and may be reached either from the north or south via Route 8 to Beacon Falls Center. Cross the Naugatuck River on an iron bridge to the west bank. From the bridge, turn right and cross a railroad overpass; turn right onto Cold Spring Road. From the railroad overpass, follow Cold Spring Road north 1.1 miles to the picnic area on the left.

Park your car in the designated area. From the northwest corner of the picnic area, follow the trail afoot, ascending northwest. At one time this trail was properly blazed, but it is now poorly marked and in need of new blazing. The lack of blazes should not pose any problems as the trail is quite well defined. As you ascend, if in doubt at any junction of the trail, keep left.

Attaining the peak, you may wish to explore, lunch, and rest

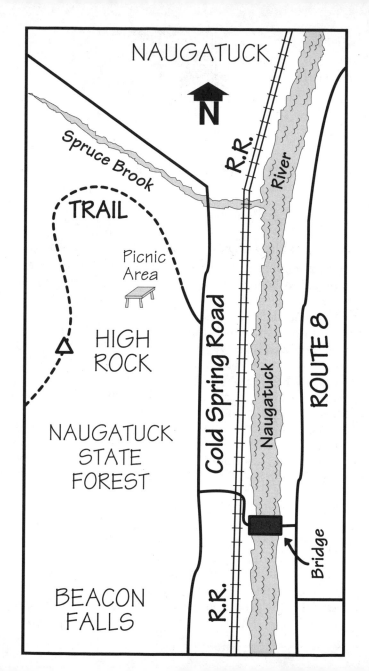

on top of High Rock before descending. Or you may travel light, leaving lunch and other gear in the car, then climbing to the crest and returning to the picnic area to enjoy lunch.

No matter where you roam in Connecticut, you will find sassafras trees growing. The white oak is Connecticut's official state tree, but the sassafras is perhaps more intimately known and recognized. It is a small tree, seldom growing taller than 40 feet or more than 2 feet in diameter. Its trunk bark is deeply furrowed and red-brown in color; the twigs are bright green. It may be immediately identified by its unusual leaf patterns, being one of a few trees displaying widely differing shaped leaves on the same tree and even the same twig. Some leaves are oval and entire; others may have one lobe and resemble a mitten; and still others may have three lobes or fingers. The American sassafras tree is closely related to the camphor tree of Japan, and it also has a pungent aroma. The root bark yields the very aromatic oil of sassafras, which is used as a flavoring in many different products. At one time sassafras tea, popularly called "sass tea," was widely used as a tonic to "clear the blood."

The sassafras tree played an important role early in American colonial history. In 1602 Bartholomew Gosnold crossed the Atlantic aboard the good ship *Conrad,* landing in the vicinity of Connecticut. The following partial report was taken from the ship's records: "Sassafras trees great plenty all the island over, a tree of high price and great profit." Later, the record states, "Some Indians we encountered remained with us behinde, bearing us company every day into the woods, and help us carie our Sassafras."

Sassafras may have the distinction of being the first plant product exported from New England.

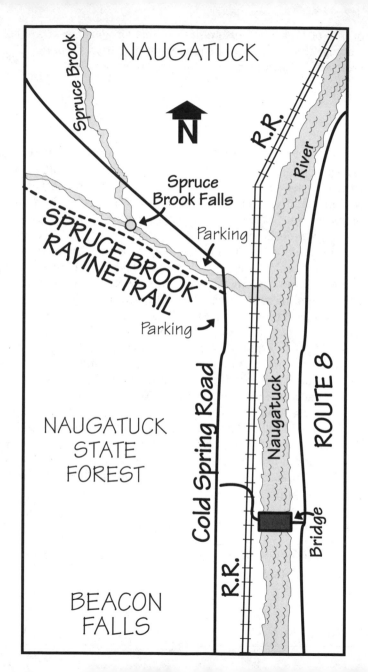

38

Spruce Brook Ravine

The largest segment of the Naugatuck State Forest lies on the west side of the Naugatuck River in the townships of Beacon Falls and Naugatuck. Spruce Brook Ravine is in the heart of this section of the forest.

To reach this beauty spot, follow the most convenient route to Route 8 in Beacon Falls, and cross the Naugatuck River on an iron bridge to the west bank. From the bridge, turn and cross the railroad overpass, turning right onto Cold Spring Road as it parallels the river and railroad and passes a picnic area on the left at 1.1 miles. Continue straight ahead .3 mile, crossing Spruce Brook to a second picnic and parking area on the left.

Park your car, then walk back across Spruce Brook to the southwest corner of the bridge where the Ravine Trail begins. The trail starts to ascend along the south bank of the brook almost immediately. The path, although sparsely blue-blazed, is well worn and easy to follow: At times it dips to the water's edge and, as suddenly, rises high above it on its course through the ravine.

Spruce Brook is considered one of the most beautiful ravines in Connecticut. No one can dispute this, but its name is a misnomer, as the early settlers incorrectly called the dense, hardy, profuse growth of hemlock in a ravine "spruce."

The trail clings closely to Spruce Brook for about .5 mile, at which point the main stream is joined by a smaller one from the west. The high point of this walk is Spruce Brook Falls, which tumbles down the rocky canyon a short distance from a juncture of the two streams.

Leave the trail and cross over to the foot of the falls. A wet foot is a small price to pay for the pleasure of exploring the falls and the precipitous canyon above it. The foot of the falls is a delightful spot to picnic or rest before retracing your steps down the trail to your car. (For a walk to High Rock, another scenic area of Naugatuck State Forest, see Walk 37.)

The experienced hiker soon learns to come to friendly enemy terms with bugs. The newcomer on the trail is apt to react to the bugs—no-see-ums, midges, gnats, deer flies, black flies, mosquitoes—as bugaboos.

There are three times as many insect species, 900,000, as all other animal species combined. The first insects appeared 250 million years before man, who made his first appearance less than one million years ago.

Man boasts of being the only thinking animal; yet, unless he soon does some real thinking and doing, he may become as extinct as the gigantic dinosaurs that also became too big for their britches. It is possible, and appears probable, that insects may outlast man by another 250 million years without the aid of thinking.

Since we cannot hope to beat the insects, nor do we have the desire to join 'em, we must learn to tolerate them. We tried to annihilate some of the harmful ones with DDT, and because without thinking we demanded instant results, we opened a Pandora's box, releasing more havoc and harm than we were originally combating.

So learn to enjoy the trails even during fly-time by using an insect repellent (see the precautions regarding Lyme disease on page xii), and try not to allow the bugs to bug you.

39

Mad River

Of all the trails in the Connecticut Blue Trail System, none excels the Mattatuck. The trail starts in the town of Wolcott and tends in a northwesterly direction for 35 miles to Mohawk Mountain in the town of Cornwall, where it joins the Appalachian Trail. Mattatuck Trail passes many beautiful lakes and streams and crosses two interesting mountains, Prospect and Mohawk.

To reach the beginning of the Mattatuck Trail, take the most convenient route to the intersection of Routes 69 and 322 in the town of Wolcott. From the signal light at this junction, follow Route 69 northeast .2 mile to Mad River Road.

On the northwest corner of Mad River Road and Route 69 is a trail marker, the standard blue oval sign lettered in white with the trail name. At this corner turn northwest onto Mad River Road, and drive .2 mile to Peterson Memorial Park, on the right.

Park your car in the parking area and follow the blazed trail, which runs along the left side of the parking lot and a fence before entering scrub growth and woodland. The trail is well worn and clearly blazed from this point. It shortly joins the Mad River and follows along its banks for almost a mile, passing several falls, cascades, and deep pools. The river banks are heavily overgrown with hemlock.

A dense hemlock forest dominates the entire area. To roam

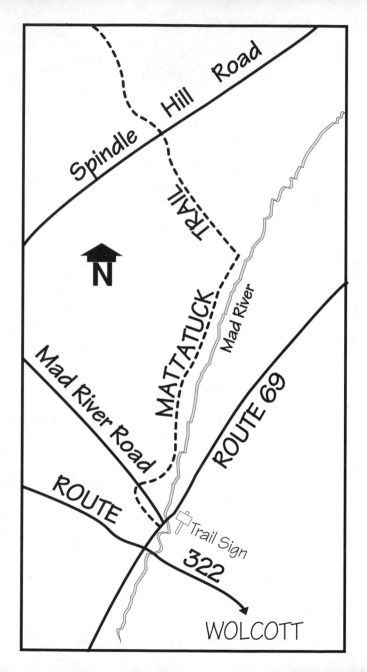

this trail is an experience that is apt to bring back the familiar lines from Longfellow's "Evangeline": "This is the forest primeval. . . . The murmuring pines and hemlocks, . . . Bearded with moss, and in garments green, indistinct in the twilight, . . . Stand like Druids of old, with voices sad and prophetic . . ."

Continue to follow the trail as it twists and turns with the babbling brook to where it leaves the stream. You may wish to turn back at this point. The river banks offer many interesting spots to explore. There are delightful ravines where one may rest, lunch, or picnic.

Since this walk is overshadowed by the vast spread of hemlock trees, perhaps a little data about the hemlock will be of interest.

The dictionary informs us that the hemlock is a tree of the coniferous genus *Tsuga canadensis*, especially a tree of eastern North America.

Hemlock trees often attain a height of 130 feet and a diameter of 3 feet or more. Hemlock seeds are eaten by several kinds of birds, and deer browse the branchlets in winter.

The early settlers made a tea from the twigs and leaves; it was given to induce sweating. New England housewives made brooms from the branchlets and often used the tender new growth for bedding.

The Eastern hemlock was one of the important trees in the original New England forests. While sufficient white pine was available, hemlock was second choice because of its brittle, splintery, usually knotty wood. Its chief importance was its bark, which was used for tanning leather, but this industry has disappeared. Now it has become an acceptable timber tree, used for cheap construction, crating, and pulpwood.

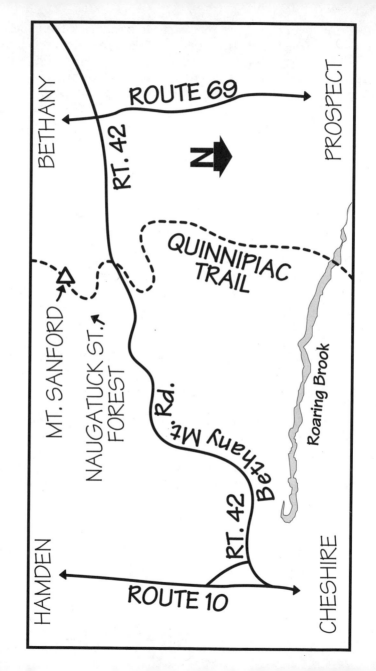

40

Roaring Brook Falls

Tensions and anxieties are not easy to eliminate from our lives, but it is wise to try. Just a change of pace on weekends helps. To crowd into the family car and then crowd in as many miles as time will permit to reach a distant attraction is not the solution. All too often we find that this creates other crises and multiplies our tensions.

Too many of us have forgotten how to enjoy life at a walking pace. We are all too familiar with the advice to slow down and seek a little isolation, but seldom do we know how to accomplish this.

One way to enjoy a leisurely walk, deep in the woods and in touch with nature, is to use one of the many blue-blazed trails maintained by the Connecticut Forest and Park Association. These trails may be reached from any point in the state in a very short time.

Roaring Brook Falls is in the town of Cheshire, on the northern portion of the Quinnipiac Trail. To reach the blue trail leading to this isolated natural beauty spot, take Route 42, an east-west highway between Cheshire and Bethany. From Route 10 in Cheshire, follow Route 42 west for 2.8 miles to where the blue trail crosses; or from Route 69 in Bethany drive east on Route 42 1.2 miles to where the trail crosses the road. The crossing is indicated by blue blazes.

Park your car off the traveled portion of the highway. Take the blue-blazed trail from Bethany Mountain Road (Route 42) to the north. The trail ascends from the road to a rise of 130 feet, or to an elevation of 720 feet above sea level. At this point the trail enters the Naugatuck State Forest and follows the boundary line between Cheshire and Prospect. It continues north, passing over several high ridges with occasional lookouts presenting views to the east, the west, and the southern skyline, dominated by towering Sanford Mountain (880 feet). The trail reaches Roaring Brook Falls 1.4 miles from Route 42.

After a moderate walk of almost 1.5 miles, you reach the glen in which Roaring Brook Falls is found—a delightful spot to rest and picnic. The whole family will enjoy this peaceful wooded area, with its gurgling falls and murmuring brook.

On the Roaring Brook section of the Quinnipiac Trail is a short run of difficult footing, a jumble of rubble and tumbled boulders on a sidehill that should be negotiated with care and proper shoes. The best shoe to wear is ankle-high, with leather uppers and thick composition soles; leather soles are apt to become slippery, especially downhill on dry leaves.

Today's way of life is one of constant pressures, yet the safety valve may be as simple as a short walk, a communion with nature.

All members of the family, from the youngest to the eldest, may take part in these walks. It requires little planning and but a short drive to the trail. A relaxing walk within the limits of the group may prove to be the pause that recreates.

Sleeping Giant

There is no need to sell all that we have to obtain that "one pearl of great price" as the biblical merchant did, seeking the kingdom of heaven.

We already have a pearl of great price in the possession of the Sleeping Giant State Park. Certainly no urban area could be more fortunate than New Haven in the possession of this treasure, the Sleeping Giant. Among the many other jewels to be found in this park at the city's very doorstep is the Nature Trail.

The Sleeping Giant State Park, comprised of more than 1,400 acres, is located mostly in the town of Hamden. The main entrance to the park is on Mount Carmel Avenue, at approximately .2 mile from Whitney Avenue (Route 10); here is to be found the ranger's headquarters and picnic areas as well as parking. Camping is no longer permitted. From this point many of the major trails start, as does the Nature Trail. All trails are indicated by a particular blaze, either by a color or a round, square, triangular, or diamond-shaped marker. The Nature Trail is indicated by painted green circles with a dark pine tree in the center or by green circles with study-station numbers.

Park your car in the designated area. Near the parking lot is a large wooden sign with a glassed-in map of the park. Also available here (except when supplies run out) are free park map folders and copies of the free booklet, *Self-Guiding Nature Trail in*

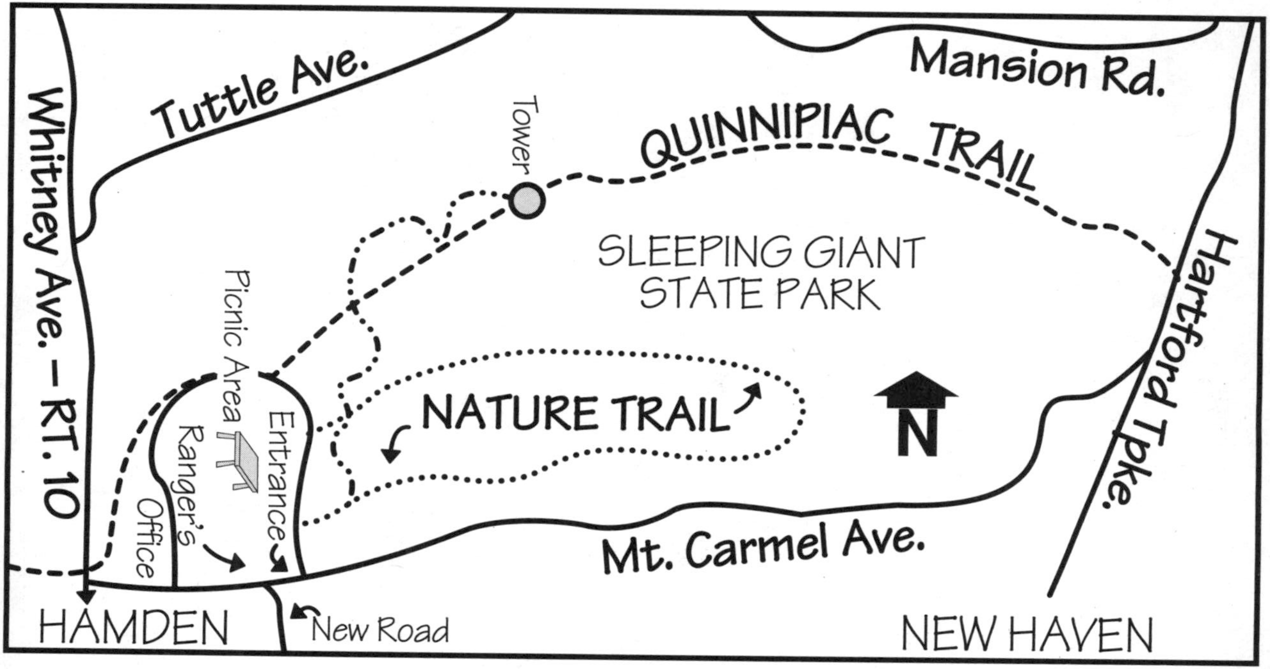
Mansion Rd.
Tuttle Ave.
Whitney Ave. – RT. 10
QUINNIPIAC TRAIL
Tower
SLEEPING GIANT
STATE PARK
Hartford Tpke.
Picnic Area
NATURE TRAIL
N
Entrance
Ranger's
Office
Mt. Carmel Ave.
HAMDEN
New Road
NEW HAVEN

Sleeping Giant State Park, which is published by the Sleeping Giant Association.

The Nature Trail is an easy, basic education in many things: geology, biology, botany, ecology. Walking it will give you a better, clearer understanding of what to look for and what you are looking at in the park.

The entire trail requires about one hour of leisurely walking; it is about 1.5 miles in length. The first part is easy, level walking and can be done by anyone, even small children or elderly persons. The last part of the trail, after the turn near the giant white pine tree, is rougher and steeper. Some may wish to return from here. (To return, go left near marker 17.)

The numbered trees and rocks beside the trail are matched with the numbered paragraphs in the *Nature Trail Guide.* The guide covers a multitude of things: trees, ferns, glacial plains, gullies, and erosion; the difference between traprock and sandstone; and much more.

The National Wildlife Federation urges every citizen to consider the vital need for outdoor recreation. "As America's population increases and more leisure time becomes available, open spaces near expanding metropolitan areas become ever more important. We must protect and preserve our rivers, forests, and seashores. To preserve the American way of life, we must first preserve America."

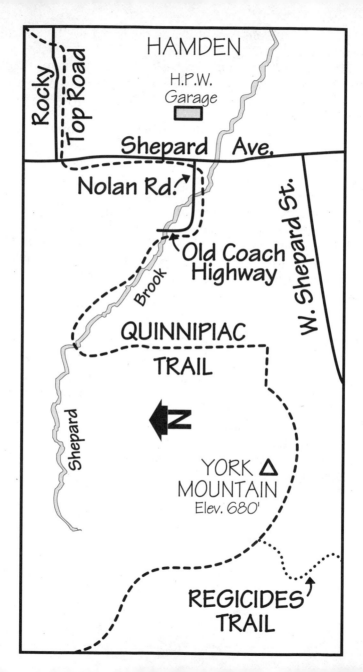

York Mountain

Some of the finest panoramic views in the state are to be had from York Mountain in Hamden. Its crest, 680 feet high, is crossed by the Quinnipiac Trail and may be reached, via trail, from the east by way of Shepard Avenue (from which point the ascent to the mountain's top is fairly steep but only 1.2 miles long).

To reach the starting point of this walk, follow the most convenient route to Nolan Road, which is west of Shepard Avenue and directly west of the Hamden Public Works garage. Nolan Road is .1 mile south of Rocky Top Road and .3 mile north of West Shepard. (To reach Shepard Avenue, go west on Westwood Avenue, which leaves Route 10 just north of the sign for Sleeping Giant State Park, at Mt. Carmel Avenue.)

Park your car, then follow the blue-blazed trail, which enters the woods from Old Coach Highway. It heads northwest, crossing and paralleling Shepard Brook. Double your enjoyment of this walk by closely exploring the brook as it tumbles and cascades down to the ponds below. The trail passes the remains of what appears to be two cabin sites before turning sharply south to follow a road .4 mile; here the trail leaves the road at a right angle, west, and ascends steeply the east face of York Mountain. This ascent is abrupt—rising some 300 feet in less than .5 mile.

To take advantage of an extensive bare rock area where one

has unobstructed views of the south and the west, the trail follows the south rim of the mountain, about 20 feet below its peak. This outcropping of rock makes the ideal place to rest and lunch while enjoying the fine vistas of the valley below.

The top of York Mountain is approximately 2.4 miles round-trip from Shepard Avenue. Should you wish to extend your walk, you may follow the main trail west to its junction with the Regicides Trail, which descends the steep south side of the mountain to Baldwin Drive, or continue north on the Quinnipiac Trail before turning back.

Walking woodland trails is an uplifting, stimulating experience at any season. Spring, the first season of our year, may be the most rewarding and inspiring due to the evidence of new life, a time of rebirth and resurrection.

The skunk cabbage thrusts her hooked nose through the yet cold, stiff muck into the business of the world above. The piping of the peepers is a welcome heralding of favorable things to come. The red-winged blackbird's crackling call comes from the reeds in the marshes. The long hibernation of the wasps, yellow jackets, and bumblebees is broken as they come forth, already pregnant, to start new colonies. The clustering honeybees leave the hive on cleansing flights and short foraging expeditions.

Spring has always evoked songs and poems of joy, none more eloquent than that fragment of Solomon's Song of Songs—"For, lo, the winter is past, the rain is over and gone; . . . The flowers appear on the earth; the time of the singing of birds is come, and the voice of the turtle-dove is heard in our land."

43

Southford Falls

Of all the Connecticut state parks, none has more to offer in natural beauty and historic lore than Southford Falls State Park. The 120 acres of which the park is comprised were acquired by the state in 1932 and 1948.

Most of the park's land lies in the township of Oxford, but the entrance and ranger headquarters are in Southbury. Eight Mile Brook is the boundary line between these two towns in the area of the park.

To reach the entrance to Southford Falls State Park, drive to the south junction of Routes 67 and 188 in Southbury. From this junction follow Route 188 southwest .4 mile to the park entrance and picnic area on the east side of the highway. Enter the parking area, leave your car, and prepare to explore the many features of the park on foot. The park trails, worn and obvious, may be followed easily with moderate attention and observation.

The most popular walk is to cross the dam at the south end of Paper Mill Pond to the east bank of Eight Mile Brook, as it falls and cascades swiftly down the deep, rocky ravine. Continue on the path close to stream, to the southwest corner of the state park's property. From here you can retrace your steps or continue on to visit the lookout tower and then loop back to the start. (Note that the map also shows two shorter loop trails.)

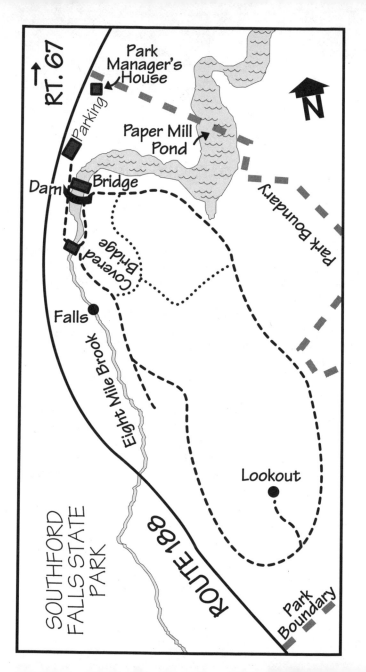

In the days of water power, Southford Falls, with its constant and powerful flow, was the site of several important mills. Perhaps the most successful of all was the Diamond Match Company's, which recycled old paper and rags to make matchbooks and matchboxes. This once-booming mill was destroyed by fire in 1923.

Early in the nineteenth century, one of man's most important inventions was conceived. In its way and for that period it was a great step forward, an advance perhaps as beneficial to mankind as the electric switch was in the twentieth century. This world-shaking achievement was the perfecting and manufacture of the friction match.

The friction match, also known as the lucifer, locofoco, kitchen, wood, or sulphur match, made flint and steel and other crude fire starters obsolete. No other animal except man has ever been able to control and maintain fire. Until the invention of the friction match, man found his methods of igniting fire slow and cumbersome. He therefore tried to keep his fires or its embers glowing, quite often a difficult and frustrating task.

In 1834 Thomas Sanford of Beacon Falls perfected the friction match, which was soon in such demand that Sanford found it necessary to increase production. He moved to Bladen Brook in Woodbridge and built a waterwheel too big for the brook to turn. Every penny Sanford had in the world went into the folly of that mammoth waterwheel, and when he failed he was so discouraged he offered to sell his match "recipe" for ten dollars. The Diamond Match Company later bought the formula and made the wooden match a commercial success.

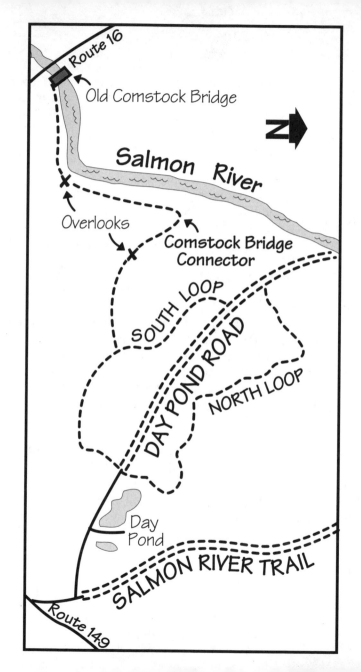

Day Pond–Salmon River

In colonial times the Day family created a pond to provide water for a sawmill, where they turned chestnut, maple, and oak logs into lumber. In the nineteenth century horses hauled wagons across the covered Comstock Bridge, over the Salmon River. Today Day Pond State Park, in Colchester, and the nearby Comstock Bridge are places to relax and enjoy with no thoughts of back breaking toil. For those who love winding trails, one special way to enjoy both the pond and the bridge is to hike the distance—less than four miles—between them.

The entrance to the 180-acre park is just off Route 49, 5.5 miles west of Colchester. The pond, stocked with trout, is a hit with fishermen; it also attracts swimmers in summer and ice skaters in winter. Around the pond, shaded picnic tables invite sitting, eating, and general ease taking. The park also has a picnic shelter, restrooms (open seasonally) and convenient parking.

Hiking trails wend through the park and the adjoining Salmon River State Forest. Most popular is the blue-blazed Salmon River Trail. One 2-mile section of it loops north of the main park road; another 2-mile loop is to the south. From the southern loop, a connecting trail leads down to the weathered Comstock Bridge, built in the 1870s.

The southern loop starts, rather ignominiously, behind some outhouses on the far side of Day Pond. In a mile and a half, it passes a pipeline easment—an open, rocky stretch. Just beyond the easement, a little wooden sign points left to the Comstock Bridge. (Beyond the sign, the regular trail continues back to the park road.)

The connector trail heads through woods and then follows a bank high above the Salmon River, with wonderful views of the sloping bank (often bright with wildflowers), the bubbling river, and the hills beyond.

The trail then descends to the bridge, which hasn't carried traffic for more than 60 years but is still maintained by the Connecticut Department of Transportation. Nobody knows who the original builder was, but he used a trusswork system developed by Ithiel Town, noted bridge builder from Thompson, Connecticut.

Once some sixty covered bridges crossed Connecticut rivers and streams; today, the Comstock is one of only three that remain. Old-timers usually explained that bridges were covered for the same reason that ladies wore petticoats—to protect the underpinnings. The Comstock's underpinnings are still fine.

It's also possible to drive to the bridge, which is just off Route 16, between Cochester and East Hampton (and is marked by a sign). A parking area is located next to the bridge. Non-hikers can just enjoy the sturdy old structure; hikers often start here to follow the blue blazes "backwards," toward the park. The trail is on the far side of the bridge, on the left.

45

Lantern Hill

The western terminus of the Narragansett Trail is in the town of North Stonington, where it is joined by the Pequot Trail from the west. The Narragansett Trail is part of the Connecticut Blue Trail System, and from its western starting point, Lantern Hill, it leads in a northeasterly direction for 16 miles to the Connecticut border and reaches its eastern terminus in Rhode Island.

To reach the Lantern Hill segment of this trail, follow the most convenient route to the juncture of Route 2 with Route 214, in the town of Ledyard. This juncture is near the Ledyard–Stonington boundary line.

Turn south onto Wintechog Hill Road and follow blue blazes .2 mile to where the trail leaves the road and enters woods. Park your car, then follow the trail up a fair grade. The trail ascends to Lantern Hill on an old tote road for .4 mile, where the Pequot Trail from the right (west) junctures with the Narragansett. Continue south, ascending steeply to Lantern Hill's summit, approximately .7 of a mile from your parked car.

The crest of Lantern Hill is about 500 feet above sea level, presenting views of Block Island, Fishers Island, Montauk Point, Norwich, and the distant hills. From the trail and crest one has a fine view of the silica quarry operation that is devouring the south end of the ridge. The vein of silica, of which Lantern Hill is

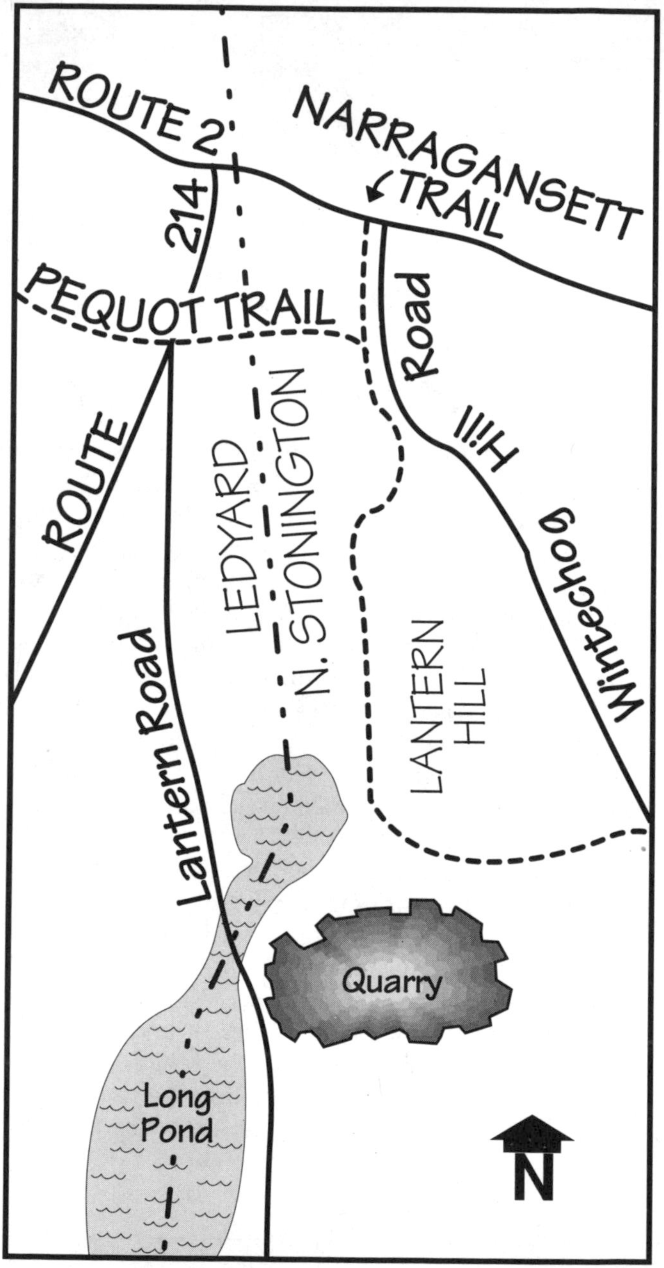

ROUTE 2
NARRAGANSETT TRAIL
214
PEQUOT TRAIL
Road
ROUTE
LEDYARD
N. STONINGTON
Hill
Wintechog
LANTERN HILL
Lantern Road
Quarry
Long Pond
N

composed, may eventually be pulverized flat by this mining operation.

Should you decide to extend your walk beyond the summit, follow the trail south and then east, descending through woods and heavy laurel growth to Wintechog Hill Road. The round-trip from your car to this point will be slightly over 2.5 miles. (For another hike on the Narragansett Trail that begins at the same starting point and heads in the opposite direction, see Walk 46.)

Back on the summit, one may view the distant scene of woods, lakes, islands, and ocean, but the predominating subject is the mining operation below. The glaring whiteness of the silica and its vast spread dazzles the senses.

The U.S. Silica Company operates the quarry on Lantern Hill Road. We are told that it is the only pure-white-silica mine in the east.

This quarry distributes nationally twenty-five grades of white aggregate, sands, and flours produced from a unique, enormous deposit of white quartz that is drilled, blasted, crushed, kiln dried, ground, screened, and air cleaned. The pure white silica is used for buildings, highways, landscaping, and glass.

The dictionary informs us that silica is silicon dioxide appearing as quartz, sand flint, and agate. The word comes from Latin *silex,* meaning flint. It does not inform us why this particular mound of pure white quartz is found here at Lantern Hill. Why should this tremendous lode of silica be massed in one hill and very little or none at all in the surrounding hills?

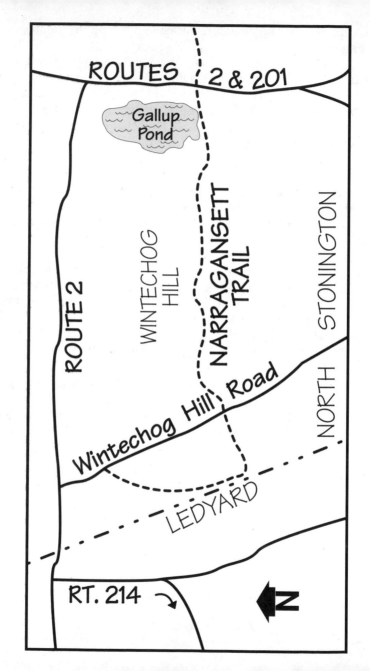

46

Wintechog Hill

The 16-mile-long Narragansett Trail starts at the Ledyard–North Stonington boundary line. It follows a northeasterly course through North Stonington and Voluntown to the Rhode Island state line.

Wintechog Hill is on the first segment at the western end of the Narragansett Trail. The trail rises and dips as it traverses the entire length of the hill, east and west, a distance of almost 2 miles.

To reach the starting point of this walk, follow road map routes to the junction of Routes 214 and 2 in the township of Ledyard. From this junction follow Route 2 east .2 mile to Wintechog Hill Road. Turn southeast onto Wintechog Hill Road and follow .8 mile to the Narragansett Trail crossing, indicated by blue-blazed trees on both sides of the road.

Park your car and follow the blazed trail east (left) along a well-defined woods road through lovely laurel. The trail bears right shortly, then bears left at the height of land and follows an old stone boundary. Emerging from the woods, it descends and follows the south border of a field until it reaches Gallup Pond and combined Routes 2 and 201.

The pond may be crossed on the dam at its south end. The round-trip from Wintechog Hill Road to Gallup Pond and return is about 3.6 miles. You may do all of it or return to your car from any point you wish. Or you may want to try Walk 45, which begins at the same starting point and heads in the opposite direction.

Appropriately, the main trails of the Connecticut Blue Trail System have been given Indian names. The two major trails in southeastern Connecticut are named for the Narragansett and Pequot Indians who lived, hunted, and roamed in this area. There is slight doubt that parts of the present blue trails were used by these Native Americans.

Indian trails crisscrossed the state in every direction. None, however, compared in importance for both Indian and colonist than the "Old Connecticut Path" and the "Shore Path." These two well-established routes crossed Connecticut: the one through the center and the other close to the shoreline.

The "Old Connecticut Path" led west to the Hudson River from Hartford and east to Shawmut, now Boston. The "Shore Path" was perhaps more heavily traveled and of greater importance. It ran east from Manhattan to Shawmut and eventually became part of our present Route U.S. 1.

Many of our older highways follow the paths made by members of the seventeen tribes that shared Connecticut prior to 1636. Not all of these trails have been used for highways. There remain many miles of trails for the interested, historically minded hiker, who may seek them out by following the Blue Trails of Connecticut.

47

Wyassup Lake

This section of the Narragansett Trail is about midway in the 16-mile-long trail. To reach it, follow the most convenient route to North Stonington Center, just off Route 2. From the village store follow Wyassup Road north for 3.2 miles to a dead-end road on the left. Turn onto the road and follow it for .7 mile to the Wyassup Lake boat ramp and parking area.

At this point the Narragansett Trail follows the road for a short distance. One-tenth of a mile from the boat launching area, the trail turns off onto a woods road. The trail follows this road for .2 mile, where it leaves the woods road and continues straight ahead for another .7 mile to High Ledge Lookout, with a fine view across Wyassup Lake to Westerly and the ocean.

If you wish to extend your walk, follow the blazed trail from the lookout for 1.4 miles through hemlock growth to Bullet Ledge, where interesting caves are found on the western side. This viewpoint is reached after a short, steep climb to the summit, about 50 feet off the main trail. (The view from Bullet Ledge is not too impressive, since it is surrounded on all sides by higher hills.) The round-trip return to your car from this point will be approximately 4.5 miles.

After returning to your car, you may wish to explore parts of Wyassup Lake. Here, as well as on ponds of other trails, one may find the fragrant white water lily blooming all summer long.

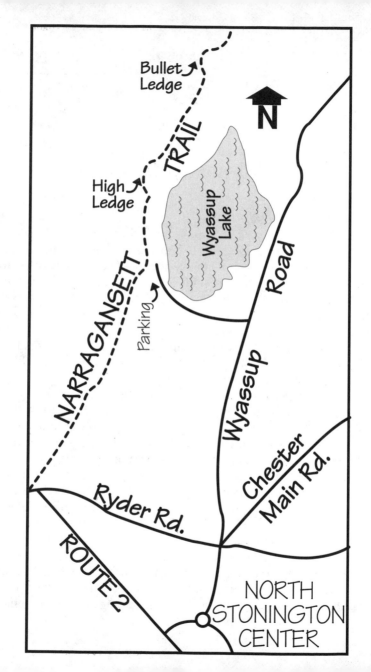

The white water lily, whose botanical name is *Nymphaea odorata*, also called water nymph, is perhaps the most beautiful of all our aquatic flowers. It is an exquisite blossom that calls for little description: a calyx of four green sepals and corolla of many petals. The petals appear to pass gradually into the stamens; it is difficult to see where the petals end and the stamens begin. Botanists seem unable to agree whether stamens are transformed petals, or petals transformed stamens. The water lily is an example of plant metamorphosis; that is, structural or functional modification of a plant organ or structure during its development.

In summer, the lily—to attract the service of insects, upon which it depends for pollination—floats fully receptive on the surface of the water. At the close of day, the lily folds its petals, pulls in stems and leaves, and silently disappears beneath the surface: just the reverse of a deep-sea diver whose lifeline is hauled out of the water at the end of the day's labors down under.

Henry David Thoreau, a keen observer of nature, had this to say about the lily, "Again I scent the white water-lily, and a season I have waited for is arrived. It is the emblem of purity and its scent suggests it. Growing in stagnant and muddy water, it bursts up so pure and fair to the eye and so sweet to the scent, as if to show us what purity and sweetness reside in, and can be extracted from the slime and muck of earth. What confirmation of our hopes is in the fragrance of the water-lily! I shall not so soon despair of the world for it."

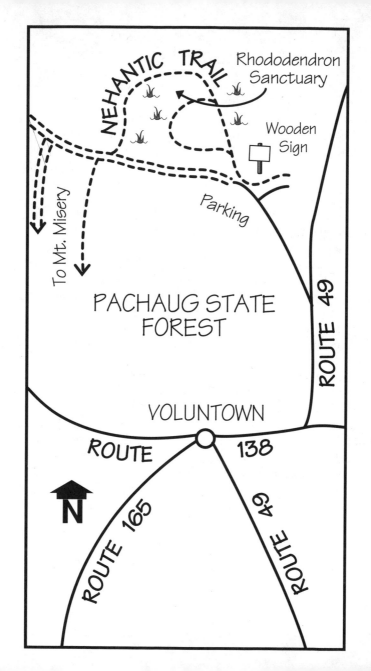

48

Rhododendron Sanctuary

The pleasure of any activity is greatly increased if it is something we really wish to do rather than because someone thinks we should. These short walks are to be done when you feel like taking one and for no other purpose than that you wish to do it.

Most rules have exceptions, and the above is no exception. The rule should be broken when planning the Rhododendron Sanctuary walk. We are told that one must visit this sanctuary between June 15 and July 15, as it is during this period that the flowers of this shrub will be in full bloom.

The Rhododendron Sanctuary is located in the Mount Misery Cedar Swamp of the Pachaug State Forest in Voluntown, Connecticut. Follow road map routes to Voluntown where Routes 49, 138, and 165 intersect. From the intersection, take combined Routes 49, 138, and 165 east for .9 mile to where Route 49 turns north. Turn onto Route 49 and follow for .7 mile to the entrance of Pachaug State Forest. From the entrance, follow the park road to a parking area near the wooden H.H. CHAPMAN sign. Park your car here. To the east of the parking area is a section of the Nehantic Trail that makes a loop through the heart of the Rhododendron Sanctuary and returns to the forest read. (A smaller loop returns to the rhododendron trail itself.)

Here in Mount Misery Cedar Swamp, the great rhododendron grows naturally and profusely. It flowers in late June and early July; its woody, fibrous branches, reaching up almost 20 feet, are so thickly interlaced that it is impossible to pass through this jungle-like barrier.

Whether the rhododendron is in bloom or not, seeing this evergreen shrub growing wild in Connecticut is a rare phenomenon. Seeing it when the blossoms are at their peak will be doubly thrilling.

"To come upon the haunts of the great rhododendron in the moist shady woods of summer is to get an inspiration that can be recalled with pleasure during the whole lifetime. For the imagination can picture no more glorious burst of nature than that which will then be spread out before you." This flowery description was written by an anonymous writer some seventy years ago.

After investigating the swamp via the blue-blazed self-guiding trail, you may wish to rest or picnic at the parking area, where you will find tables, benches, and restrooms. This area is part of 2,000 acres of the Pachaug Forest dedicated on May 21, 1966, as a memorial to the late Professor Herman Haupt Chapman of the Yale School of Forestry for his interest in Connecticut's natural resources.

As unique as the Rhododendron Sanctuary may be, Pachaug Forest also has other unusual and rare plants that should be of interest to many—not for the pleasure of the botanist alone but for the enjoyment of the novice as well. Here one can find bearberry, a trailing evergreen shrub bearing small, bright red berries; inkberry, a shrub with leather evergreen leaves and black berries; sundews, insect-eating bog plants; royal ferns with tall, upright fronds; and the ostrich fern, resembling small ostrich plumes growing in a graceful circle from an erect rootstock.

Note: This walk is very near Walk 49, Mount Misery.

49

Mount Misery

Pachaug State Forest is the largest of all the Connecticut state forests. It is comprised of about 24,000 acres, most of which lie in the towns of Griswold, North Stonington, and Voluntown. This forest has much to offer: hiking, camping, boating, swimming, forest development, botany, geology, ecology, and bridle paths.

The Pachaug Trail is approximately 30 miles long; its east terminus is Beach Pond on the Connecticut–Rhode Island state line, and its west, Pachaug Pond in Griswold. Of the many outstanding features on this trail, perhaps the one high spot literally and figuratively is Mount Misery.

The blue-blazed trail that passes over Mount Misery is the combined Pachaug and Nehantic Trail, joined together for 2.2 miles to follow the same course over the mountain.

To reach the combined trail starting on the east side of the mountain, take the forest road north of Route 138 at the Griswold–Voluntown boundary line. The forest road is .5 mile west of Voluntown center on Route 138, just west of the electric sub station on Sawmill Pond.

Turn north onto the forest road (dirt); pass through the state forest gate and continue 1.7 miles to a ball park and camping area. Turn left (northwest) and follow the road .2 mile to a trail entrance, indicated by blue-blazed trees.

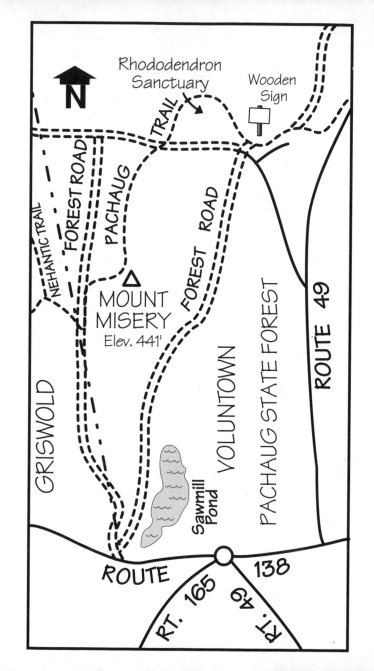

Park your car off the traveled portion of road. Follow the blue-blazed trail south through heavy hemlock growth and ascend to a ledge with a fine view. From this ledge the trail drops to a brook before ascending steeply to the summit of Mount Misery, 441 feet high. The top of Mount Misery is partly bald rock, from which one may take in the far-flung views of the eastern hills and ridges of Connecticut and Rhode Island.

Depending on the length of walk one wishes to take, the trail may be retraced from here or continued by descending quite abruptly to the west base of the mountain and then to the separating of the trails, Pachaug south and Nehantic north, at about .5 mile from the peak of Mount Misery.

We are fortunate in the possession of Pachaug State Forest with its unusual and rare finds of botanical and geological specimens. To the delight of any botanist, here are to be found the great rhododendrons, the Atlantic white cedar, and bearberry false heather, all rare plants for Connecticut. In this area the geologist will find kettle holes in the streams and well-defined ridges known as eskers. Eskers are serpentine ridges of sand and gravel believed to have been formed 20,000 years ago by streams under or in the glacial ice. It is assumed that the action of glacial drift was responsible for the botanical and geological conditions we find here today.

When we realize that the shifting of myriad grains of sand through eons of time brought about these things we now view with fascination, we more readily understand the Biblical admonition, ". . . be not ignorant of this one thing, that one day is with the Lord as a thousand years, and a thousand years as one day."

Note: This walk is very near Walk 48, Rhododendron Sanctuary.

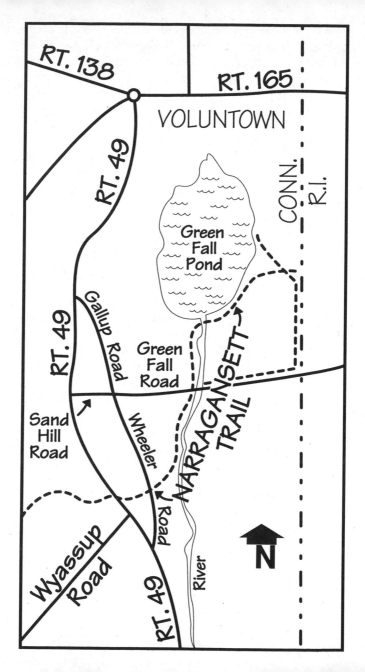

Green Fall Pond

Green Fall Pond is in Voluntown on the Narragansett Trail, which terminates at the Connecticut–Rhode Island boundary about 1 mile east of the pond.

The section of the trail leading to Green Fall Pond may be reached from Voluntown's Routes 49, 138, and 165; from this junction follow Route 49 south 4.6 miles to Sand Hill Road. Approaching from the south, follow Route 49 north to Wyassup Lake Road. The First Baptist Church is on the northwest corner. At this point the Narragansett Trail crosses Route 49 and is marked with the customary oval trail sign. Continue north on Route 49 1.1 miles to Sand Hill Road.

Turn east onto Sand Hill Road and follow it for .9 mile to a junction of Gallup Road north, Wheeler Road south, and Green Fall Road east. Follow Green Fall Road east .8 mile to the trail crossing, indicated by blue-blazed trees.

Park your car off the traveled portion of the road and follow the self-guiding trail north. Descending from the road, the trail shortly reaches Green Fall River and follows it upstream through a beautiful ravine densely covered with hemlock.

The trail clings to the river for .5 mile before reaching the dam at Green Fall Pond. It crosses the dam to the east, following the shoreline for .7 mile, then enters the woods, zig-zagging past a shelter to an old mill site. Passing through a heavily concentrated blueberry bush area, the trail junctures with a side trail about 1.5 miles from Green Fall Pond. The side trail leads northwest .1 mile to an exposed ledge with a view across inland marsh. Retrace the side trail to the main trail and follow it east to the Connecticut state line. Follow the trail south along the boundary line to a massive boulder and rock outcropping with a cave underneath. The trail continues south to Green Fall Road, where the Connecticut portion of the Narragansett Trail ends. The Rhode Island portion of the trail is yellow-blazed.

Turn right (west) on Green Fall Road and follow it 1 mile to your parked car. The completed loop is approximately 3.7 miles long, not including the side trail.

This is one of the more delightful trails in the entire Connecticut Blue Trail System. The rainforest-like ravine; waterfalls; placid ponds; the variety of trees, flowers, and birds are compensation for the heavy activity of nature lovers in this area, especially during school vacation.

This activity, which you may find slightly disturbing, is caused by the general appeal of the area and primarily because of the popularity of Yawgoog Pond, just over the line in Rhode Island. There are many organizations using the Yawgoog Pond area as a summer campground. The trails in the vicinity of Green Fall Pond and Yawgoog Pond are apt to be used by organized groups of summer campers. Do not be surprised if you suddenly encounter a boisterous gaggle of children.

This, too, is a part of nature, and the philosophical hiker seeking relaxation and solitude must accept it or use this section of the trail system only during periods when schools are in session.

51

Nathan Hale Forest

Nathan Hale was born in 1755 in a house on his family's property in Coventry, Connecticut. In 1776 Nathan's father built a new house on the property; that house, known as the Hale Homestead, is now a museum operated by the Antiquarian and Landmarks Society (742–6917). It is open to the public from mid-May to mid-October. (An admission fee is charged.)

The homestead property adjoins the Nathan Hale State Forest, which comprises some 1,219 acres and lies within the townships of Andover and Coventry. The homestead is outside the eastern boundary of the forest. Both homestead and forest were donated to the present custodians through the generosity of George Dudley Seymour.

The Hale Homestead may be reached easily from two directions. From the north, drive to the junction of Daly Road and Route 31, about midway between Coventry and South Coventry. The junction is near the northwest end of Wangumbaug Lake. Follow Daly Road south 1.3 miles to South Street. Turn right onto South Street and follow it west .5 mile to Nathan Hale's birthplace. Approaching from the south, drive to the junction of Routes 316 and U.S. 6 in Andover. From the junction follow Route U.S. 6 west .4 mile to Long Hill Road; turn north onto Long Hill Road and follow it 2 miles to Skinner Hill Road. Bear right, east, and follow Skinner Hill Road 1.1 miles to South

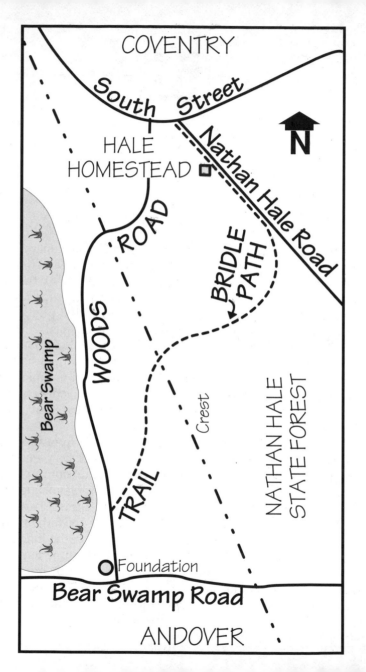

Street. Turn right, southeast, onto South Street and follow it .5 mile to Nathan Hale's birthplace.

There are numerous trails, bridle paths, and woods roads open to the hiker. You might choose to start on a dirt road some 250 feet west of the maple grove on South Street, to the west of the homestead. The road goes left, then right, and reaches an open area at about .5 mile. A trail from the right-hand corner of the open area leads over a ridge above Bear Swamp. Continue south on this ridge to the southern end of the state forest and Bear Swamp Road, where an old house foundation (barely visible) marks the northwest corner. You may wish to rest and picnic here before retracing your steps back to your car. This point is approximately 1.25 miles from the homestead.

An alternate return route for the adventuresome is via trail and bridle path on the crest east of the lower ridge. From the old house foundation a short distance north on a woods road is an overgrown trail on the right, not blazed, ascending steeply to the north. At the Andover–Coventry boundary line, the trail turns east to Nathan Hale Road, which is unimproved. Follow this road northwest to return to your car. The round-trip for either route will be about 3 miles.

The highlights of Nathan Hale's life and supreme sacrifice are well-known. To walk over the same ground he trod as a boy cannot help but remind us of two distinct revolutionary periods in our history: then and now. History repeats itself. Then there were protesters, deserters, and selfless heroes. Then, as now, men asked, "What's in it for me?," and other men only wished to know, "How much can I give?"

As we follow Nathan Hale's footsteps around the farm, we are carried by imagination to the gallows in New York where, on September 22, 1776, at 11 o'clock in the morning, he was hanged, uttering his never-to-be-forgotten last words, "I regret that I have but one life to lose for my country."

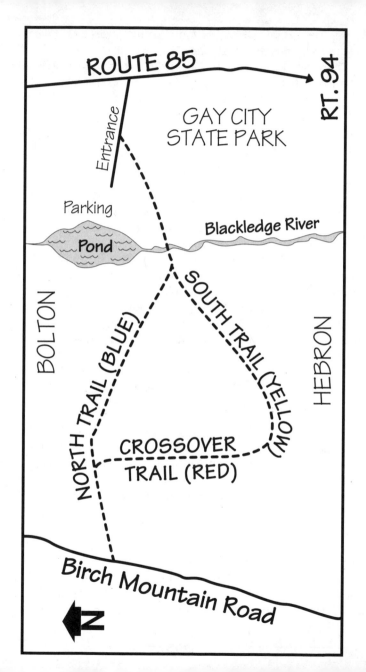

52

Gay City

A delightful network of hiking trails has been developed by the state in Gay City State Park. There are ten numbered and blazed trails, ranging from easy to not-too-difficult, coursing through the park proper as well as in the adjoining Meshomasic State Forest.

The entrance to Gay City State Park is on the west side of Route 85 in the township of Hebron. It is most easily reached from the junction of Route 94 with Route 85 in Hebron. From the junction follow Route 85 north 1.9 miles to the park entrance. Approaching from the north on Route 85, continue south from the Bolton–Hebron boundary line .7 mile to the park entrance.

Enter the park and follows signs to either of two ample parking lots near the pond. Leave your car; if the ranger is on duty, ask for a free map showing locations of the trails and other features of the area.

From the parking lot return on foot .2 mile on the surfaced entrance road to a barway across the old Gay City Road on the right. This is the eastern terminus of blue-blazed Trail #2 (North Trail). From this point follow the dirt road west, descending to Blackledge River, cross the bridge, and continue on the blue-blazed North Trail about 1 mile to Crossover Trail, blazed in red. Turn left and follow Crossover Trail south about half a mile to the junction with South Trail, blazed in yellow. Continue left on

South Trail less than a mile to return to the North Trial. After re-crossing Blackledge River, keep left, passing the ruins of the old mill. Follow the connecting path north paralleling the old aqueduct to the dam, pond, parking area, and your car.

The above walk will total about 2.5 miles. Should you wish to extend it, follow the North Trail to its juncture with the Crossover Trail, but bypass the Crossover and continue west on the North Trail for another half mile, to Birch Mountain Road. Then turn around and retrace your steps on the North Trail back to the Crossover, and continue as described above.

In 1796, a religious sect led by Elijah Andrus settled in the area that later became known as Gay City. In 1800, after Andrus's departure, John Gay was elected president of the community that soon bore his name.

The settlement of Gay City waxed and prospered and was almost self-sustaining. At its peak, the thriving colony boasted twenty-five families, with the Gay clan in the majority. There were large farms and homes, a sawmill, two grist mills, and a very successful woolen mill. There were also mills that manufactured paper and satinette.

The inhabitants of Gay City were both conscientiously industrious and religious. They had compulsory church services twice each week. One may presume that this edict was made more palatable by the custom of serving quantities of hard liquor at these services.

53

Nipmuck Trail

The well-blazed Nipmuck Trail, about 39 miles long, has two sections, totalling almost 14 miles, in Mansfield. A particularly picturesque segment follows the Fenton River and terminates at Route 44, after following Old Turnpike (dirt) and crossing Fenton River before reaching the highway.

This segment of the trail may be reached by following road map routes to Route 195 at Storrs. From Route 195 turn east onto Gurleyville Road and drive 1.4 miles to a bridge crossing the Fenton River. The blue-blazed trail crosses Gurleyville Road just west of the bridge.

Park your car and follow the trail in a northwesterly direction, passing a dense stand of old pines close to the west bank of the river.

At no time does this portion of the Nipmuck Trail reach any appreciable elevation for a distant view; it compensates by remaining close to the river's edge with its contrasting still, passive pools and rushing rapids.

One may traverse this short section of the trail in less than one hour by striding along, but the inviting nature of this trail is so appealing that one is compelled to stop constantly to admire its many features and is apt to spend many pleasant hours here. The round-trip is about 3 miles.

Sit quietly near any of the numerous bends of the river and enjoy the calling, chattering, and singing of the birds. You may

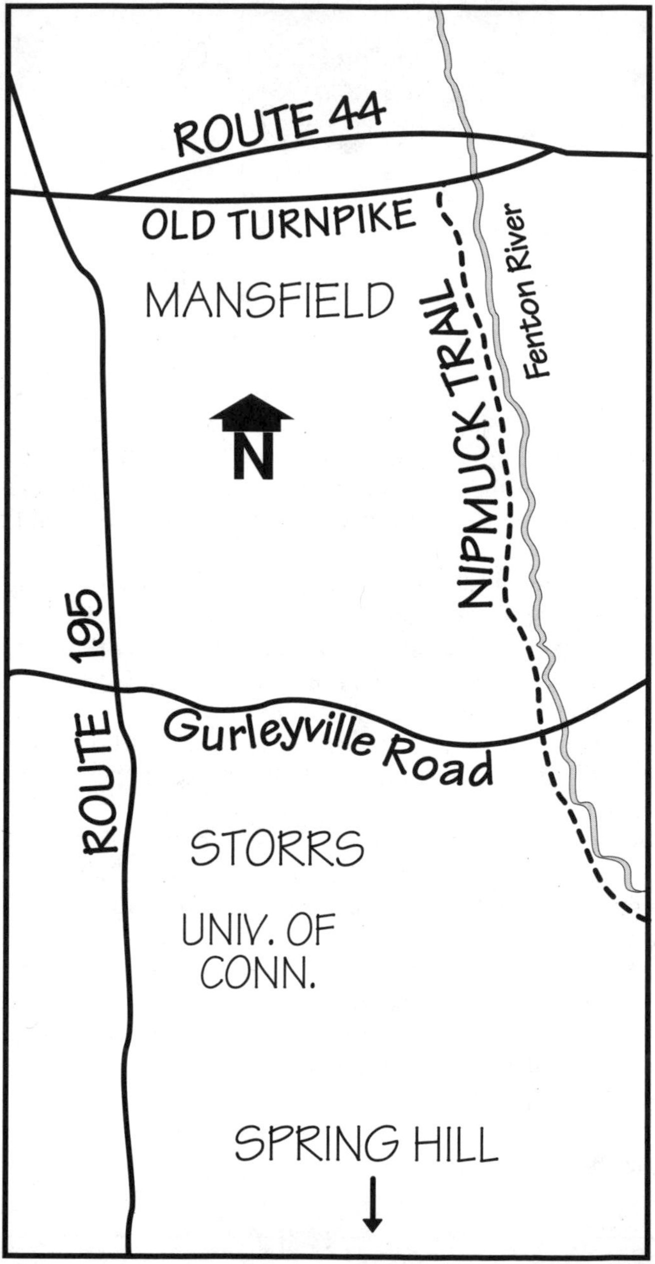
ROUTE 44
OLD TURNPIKE
MANSFIELD
N
NIPMUCK TRAIL
Fenton River
ROUTE 195
Gurleyville Road
STORRS
UNIV. OF
CONN.
SPRING HILL

also have the good fortune of seeing one of the flying squirrels reported in this area.

It is readily understandable that we would be more preoccupied with the lilting song of a bird or a squirrel gliding gracefully through the air than with a glob of the spittlebug in the grass beneath our feet. In fact, this "spit" at first sight may cause a moment of revulsion. It should not, for it is as clean and perhaps as comforting to the insect within it as a luxurious bubble bath would be to a human.

This white mass of bubbles is found on grasses so frequently that it has earned a multitude of names: bubble villa, froth castle, cuckoo-spit, frog-spit, frog-foam, foam mansion, et cetera. The bubbles are made by the females and young nymphs. The female makes the froth to cover her eggs. The babies, which resemble microscopic frogs, suck plant juices to use for food and to make their froth covering. The bubbles burst and must be constantly replaced.

Gently push the foam aside with a twig, and inside the mass you will see a small, squat, light-green, miniature frog-like insect. Why this insect develops in this frothy mass is anybody's guess. "For protection" may actually be the case, but protection from what? The nymph is so small it would take a sharp eye to detect it, but the mass of bubbles with which it surrounds itself is certainly a most obvious sign of the spittlebug's presence to any preying enemy.

Contact with simple things; the symmetry and orderliness of nature; her timelessness and serenity—these are the things that breed contentment. To walk with nature is among the most rewarding pleasures of life.

Note: From the end of this walk, the Nipmuck Trail follows Route 44 briefly, then re-enters woods. The next section of the trail, Daleville, is Walk 54.

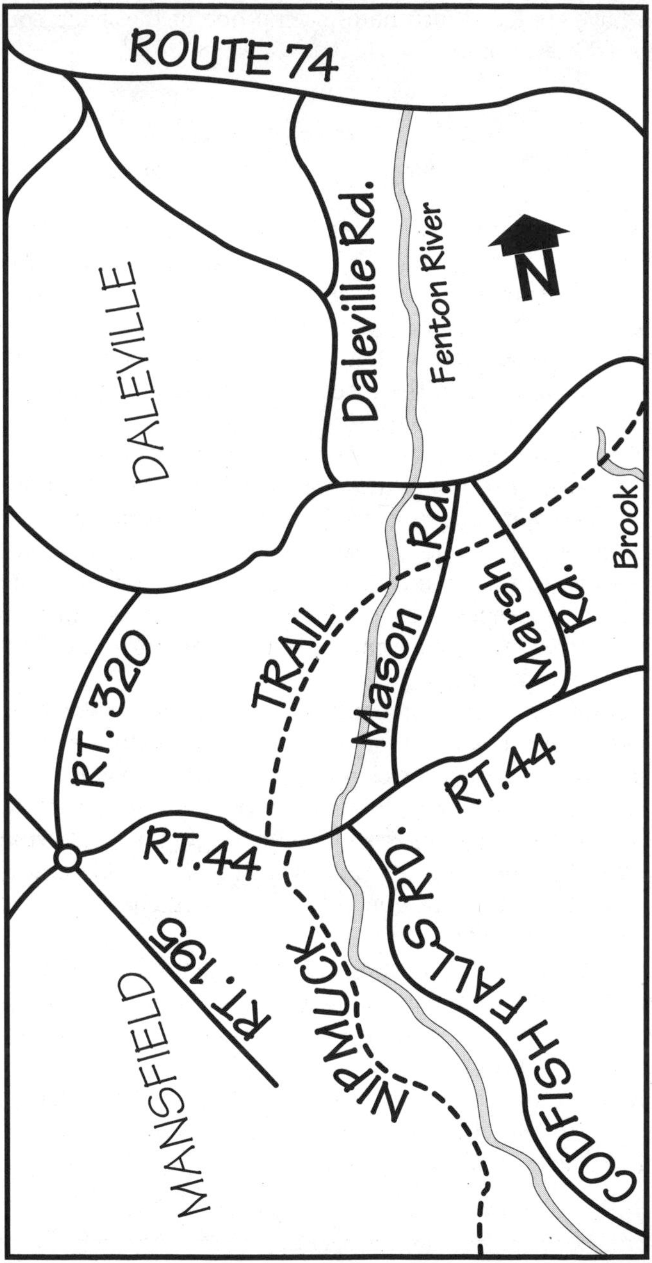
ROUTE 74
DALEVILLE
Daleville Rd.
Fenton River
N
Mason Rd.
Marsh Rd.
Brook
TRAIL
RT. 320
RT.44
RT.44
CODFISH FALLS RD.
NIPMUCK
RT. 195
MANSFIELD

Daleville

The Daleville segment of the Nipmuck Trail goes north from Route 44. The trail continues about 5 miles to Route 174, but our short walk is to visit a brook a little more than 2 miles from Route 44.

This trail section starts on the north side of Route 44, just south of the Willington/Mansfield boundary line and about .25 mile west of Codfish Falls Road.

To reach this point from the west, drive to the intersection of Routes 44, 195, and 320 in Mansfield. From the intersection follow Route 44 east 1.75 miles to Codfish Falls Road. Approaching from the east, follow the most convenient route to the junction of Routes 74 and U.S. 44 at West Ashford. From the junction follow Route 44 west 3.5 miles to Codfish Falls Road.

From Route 44 (just west of Codfish Falls Road), the blue-blazed trail, marked by the traditional oval marker, goes along a fence near a driveway. Follow the trail, with the fence on your right, along a right-of-way that leads to a natural area by the Fenton River. Continue on through a pine plantation, then follow the river until the trail veers right.

In about 1.25 mile, cross Mason Road. If you wish, you can make a right here and follow Mason Road back about .5 mile to return to Route 44.

Or keep following the trail, which in less than a mile will cross paved Marsh Road. It will later descend through the woods to a brook in a lovely hemlock grove before reaching Route 174.

The present Nipmuck Trail is about 39 miles long. The ends of its two southern branches are in Mansfield Center; the northern end of the trail extends into Bigelow Hollow State Park in Union. Long before any pioneers settled in Connecticut, the Nipmuck Trail was a well-established, important Indian trail passing north and south through the width of the state from what is now New London to Massachusetts. On its northward course it followed the west side of the Thames River to Norwich, continuing north to intersect the Old Connecticut Path, or Great Trail, in what is now Ashford.

The Great Trail ran generally east and west through Massachusetts and Connecticut between Boston and Hartford. It crossed the Nipmuck Trail just east of the present village of Warren, which was the original Ashford. It was so named because the Great Trail crossed Mount Hope River at an easy fording place that was surrounded by numerous ash trees; naturally it became known as "ash ford."

The old Nipmuck Trail was the western boundary of ancient Windham township. In 1691 the town fathers of Windham sought to fix a straight line for that boundary. This caused long and bitter arguments. The court and church made decisions and gave orders, but the controversy continued over a period of sixty years.

The dispute was settled quite simply by an imbecile. He lived in the disputed territory; Windham finally yielded in 1752 to avoid paying for his support. It would appear that the colonists also had their welfare problems.

Note: This walk is just north of Walk 53.

55

Bigelow Hollow

Most of the 8,058 acres of the Nipmuck State Forest lie in the township of Union. This forest in the northeastern part of Connecticut and close to the Massachusetts border has much to offer, not the least of which is Bigelow Hollow State Park. It is thought that the park area got its name not from any local person named Bigelow but rather from the deep hollow—or "big low"—in which Bigelow Pond is located.

The park offers excellent recreational facilities, including picnicking, boating, fishing, and hiking. To reach the main entrance to Bigelow Hollow State Park, follow the road map routes to Route 171 in Union. The entrance is on the north side of Route 171 and is approximately midway between Route 197 on the east and Route 190 on the west.

Enter the park and follow the service road; park your car in the designated area. Bigelow Pond, which has a trail around it, is entirely within the park. The park also skirts the southern shore of Mashapaug Lake, which got its name from the Nipmuck Indian word for "great pond." A trail is at the southern tip of the lake. Other trails (including the blue-blazed Nipmuck Trail) wend through the park and through adjoining land in the Nipmuck State Forest.

You may wish to lunch and rest at any of the numerous picnic tables or other spots that may appeal to you, or you may wish to explore the mixed hardwood and evergreen forest.

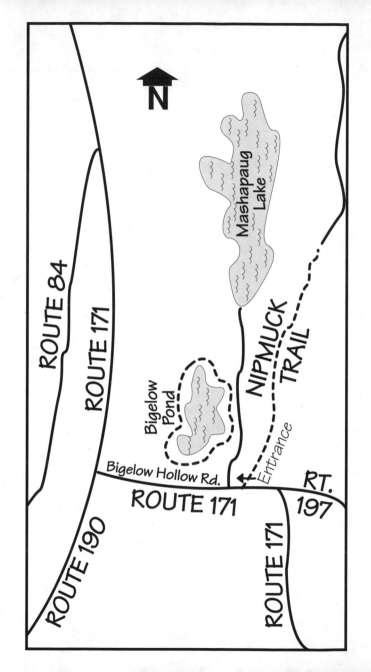

Should you desire more information about other features of this popular park, the ranger in charge will be pleased to inform you.

These short walks are not intended to break any hiking records but rather to give one an opportunity to enjoy the basic exercise of walking in relaxing surroundings. There are many things of interest to be found beside the trails: flowers, birds, trees, insects, and wildlife. One cannot help but be enthralled on any walk in the woods.

However enthralling a woodland walk may prove to be, it is doubly so when walking and exploring at the edge of a lake or pond. Even the least observant hiker must pause, reflect, and wonder when he observes the constant activity, the life-and-death struggle to survive, that is so intense around, on, and in a pond.

In spring and summer the inhabitants of a pond and its shores reach the peak of their ceaseless effort to live and grow. Nature constantly places obstacles in the way of all life with the dictum "adapt, improve, perfect, or die."

The interested observer may be presented in a few dramatic moments a chapter or several chapters from the story of the web of life in a pond. Episodes are constantly taking place: A dragonfly swoops low over the water's surface, scooping up smaller insects with its long legs, then sucking their succulent juices, only to fall victim to a frog's swiftly darting tongue; moments later the frog, jumping into the water to escape a preying snake, is gobbled up by a bass; and so on, ad infinitum.

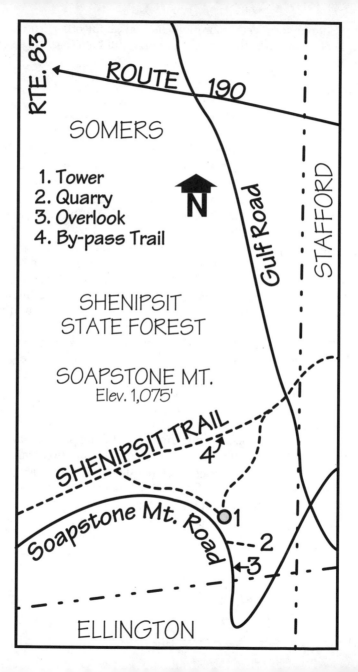

56

Soapstone Mountain

Soapstone Mountain is in the southeast corner of the township of Somers. It is close to where the boundary lines of Ellington, Stafford, and Somers join. It is also on the Shenipsit Trail and in the Shenipsit State Forest.

The crest of Soapstone Mountain, 1,075 feet above sea level, is crowned by a weather-relay station and a fire tower and offers spectacular views. Soapstone Mountain Road—paved—leads up the mountain; it is open year round during daylight hours (but may be closed by snow).

The least complicated approach to Soapstone Mountain is from the intersection of Gulf Road with Route 190 in the town of Somers. The intersection is 1.2 miles east of Route 83, using Route 190. At the intersection, turn southeast onto Gulf Road and drive almost 2 miles to an entrance to the Shenipsit State Forest. Leave your car in the parking area to proceed on foot, or continue by car, and turn west onto Soapstone Mountain Road. It ascends to a sharp hairpin turn before reaching a fine over-look at .8 mile from Gulf Road. Stop at the overlook and take in the distant views to the south and east. Near the top of the mountain is a picnic area with portable restrooms. Just beyond is the weather-relay station, closed off from the public by a wire fence. From this area, a short trail leads to the wooden fire tower behind the station.

From Soapstone Mountain Road, many connecting trails lead to interesting walks. One of these is between the tower and hairpin turn overlook; a well-worn path to the right, not blazed but easy to follow, leads to an old soapstone quarry, for which the mountain is named. You may also want to follow the trail northwest down the steep cone of the mountain to the ascent of the western peak, 930 feet high and .7 mile from the tower.

It must be assumed that those who are interested in these short walks are also interested in nature and her many offerings. But why do so many who are usually fascinated by and delight in nature's creations have a revulsion against spiders? The spider is a creature whose value most of us have not learned to appreciate. Here is a comment by one who did:

The famous nineteenth-century American arachnologist, Reverend Henry Christopher McCook, wrote the following: "Spiders are good forest keepers, defending trees and plants against the onslaughts of aphids and insects. They also help humans by keeping down mosquitoes and gnats. They, in fact, labor incessantly to check increase of the hordes of insects that otherwise would banish humans from many parts of the earth. Nor do they make reprisals of any sort for this service. They never attack fields, harvests, vineyards, or orchards like beetles, grasshoppers, and other insects in the adult and larval state. They never forage on the goodies in kitchen and pantry as do roaches and ants. They do not torment and afflict by cutting, piercing, sawing, and pumping, by buzzing, humming, and blowing like mosquito and housefly, to say nothing of less desirable entomological species. An occasional and doubtful spider bite one does hear of at rare intervals; a harmless cobweb here and there in a corner or cranny of one's house, that is all that can be charged against them. Yet they are despised, abhorred, persecuted, and slain with a zest that is hardly shown against any other creature except the snake."

57

Goodwin State Forest

All the Connecticut Blue Trails, state forests, and state parks may and should be revisited again and again. One cannot cover completely or thoroughly even the smallest area in one short walk. Each return visit will bring to light new and interesting features not discovered or seen on previous walks. Not only do the scenes change and have a different aspect as the seasons change, but something new is apt to present itself from day to day to those who are consciously observant.

Certainly the above is doubly true about the James L. Goodwin State Forest and Conservation Center. This park and forest is in the township of Hampton in Windham County. The main entrance to the Conservation Center is on the north side of Route U.S. 6, approximately 3 miles east of Route 198. Turn in on Potter Road and drive the short distance to service buildings and a parking area.

The ranger's office is in the old farmhouse, where information and maps describing the park and forest may be obtained.

The Goodwin State Forest is a wildlife sanctuary set aside to afford opportunity to all to observe the surprisingly diverse natural population of birds and other animals under natural conditions.

Enhancement of wildlife has been accomplished in the forest in many ways. Three ponds have been built on the area, the

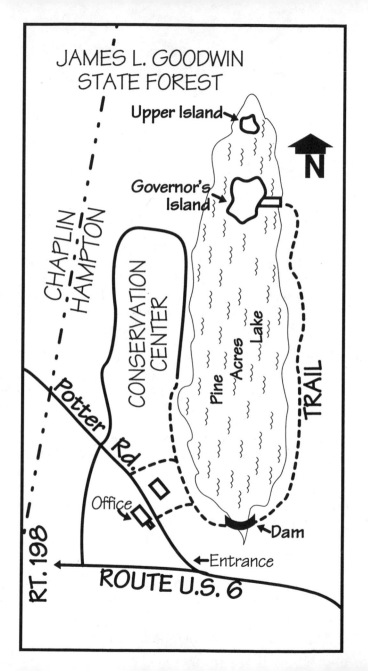

largest being Pine Acres Lake. Deer have over-wintered in the forest and are quite numerous. Beaver are active in the ponds and have been present in the forest for many years.

Although the amazing world of nature is all about us, it may best be discovered and observed on foot along woodland trails. Here all natural acts of nature rightfully appear as miracles to us. One of the infinite number of nature's miracles is the production of honey by honeybees.

Most honey, nature's perfect food, is manufactured from nectar offered by the flowers that bloom in the fields, orchards, and woods. The foraging bee visits blossom after blossom, inserting her hollow tongue into the corolla of each flower and extracting a minute droplet of nectar, which passes into the bee's honey sac, a sort of internal knapsack, directly in front of her true stomach. Having filled her honey sac to capacity, she wings her way back to the colony, where the precious cargo is regurgitated into a honey-comb cell to await further processing by hive bees. Nectar can only be changed into honey after first passing through the honey sac, where the essential jot of enzyme, the catalytic leaven, is added to the nectar before it can ripen into pure honey. The next step is taken by the hive bees, who must evaporate (by fanning) all the water from the nectar, leaving only leavened sugars. It is then sealed in the cell with a cap of wax, ready for use as food by the bees when needed.

Not only has the honeybee perfected the perfect food, she has also developed the perfect method of preserving that food.

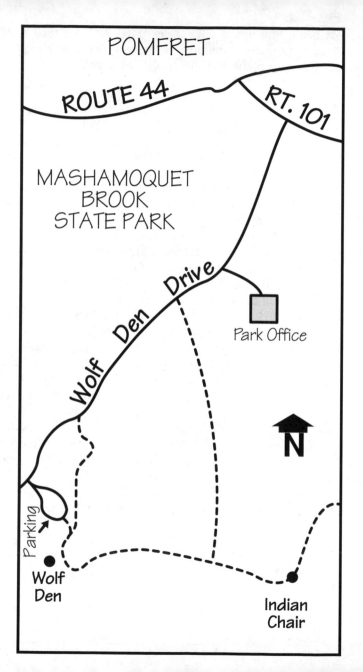

58

Putnam Wolf Den

Major General Israel Putnam was affectionately called "Old Put" by his men. He was the subject of numerous humorous as well as serious anecdotes.

Israel Putnam was born in 1718 in Danvers, Massachusetts. As a young man he moved to Pomfret, Connecticut, where he became a prosperous innkeeper and successful farmer. It is alleged that he answered the call to join the Continentals at Lexington so hurriedly that he left his plow halfway down a furrow in the middle of a field. He served conspicuously at the Battle of Bunker Hill. Promoted to major general, he commanded the American forces at the Battle of Long Island. IIe was the senior major general of the Continental Army and in command of the right wing at the time of its winter encampment in 1778–1779 at Redding, Connecticut. In 1779, when Old Put was 60, he made a dramatic mounted escape from pursuing British dragoons, riding headlong down the perilous one hundred steps carved in the precipice at Horse Neck, Greenwich.

Of all of Israel Putnam's flamboyant exploits, perhaps none is more familiar and renowned than his encounter with the wolf. For several years, Putnam and his farm neighbors were sustaining minor losses of stock due to a marauding lone wolf. But when in one night Putnam suffered a serious loss of many sheep, he vowed to get the wily killer. He enlisted the aid of five neighbors to hunt in alternating pairs. Two members of the team constantly and relentlessly trailed the wolf day after day until finally they tracked her through the snow to her lair. They tried smoking her out of the stronghold without success. They sent in the hounds; but after being severely mauled, the dogs would not reenter the cave.

In desperation, Putnam decided to squeeze through the long, low, narrow passageway to confront the "varmint" with birchbark torch and trusty smooth-bore gun. Tying a rope to his ankle, he crawled into the deep, dark dungeon, instructing his companions on the outside to drag him out pronto if he yanked the rope twice. In the excitement their signals got crossed, and they hauled him out so fast his jacket and shirt were stripped off over his head; he lost part of his breeches and much of his hide. Removing the rope, he wryly stated that he'd rather face the wolf without friendly help. After being driven back once by the wolf, he returned, shot her, then dragged the heavy carcass out by the ears.

The Putnam Wolf Den is in the Mashamoquet Brook State Park in Pomfret township. To reach the Den, drive to the junction of Route 101 with Route U.S. 44 in Pomfret. At the south side of this junction is Wolf Den Drive (largely unpaved and closed in winter), which is followed south approximately 1.75 miles to stone gateposts indicating a parking area. Leave your car and follow the trail as it descends on a gradual grade to the Wolf Den, midway down the east face of the high cliff.

After exploring the Wolf Den, continue down the trail to the Indian Chair, a naturally formed stone settee on top of a 20-foot-high stone mass. From the Chair you may retrace your steps to the Den and parking lot. Or, if you choose, you may follow another popular marked trail in the area before returning to your car.

59

Quinebaug Trail

The Quinebaug Trail is part of the Connecticut Blue Trail System. It is 5.5 miles long and lies almost entirely within the Pachaug State Forest. The northern section of this trail is in the town of Plainfield; the southern portion is in Voluntown.

The northern terminus of Quinebaug Trail is at the junction of Spaulding Road and Route 14A (Plainfield Pike). Spaulding Road is 1.6 miles east of the Connecticut Turnpike's Exit 88 on Route 14A. From the junction of Routes 14A and 49 in the town of Sterling, Spaulding Road is 1.9 miles west.

Turn south onto Spaulding Road from Route 14A and drive .4 mile to where the blue-blazed trail enters a woods road. Leave your car and proceed afoot, following the blazed trail, which is primarily a woodland trail on old tote roads. Lockes Meadow, a swampy wetland area, is about 1.9 miles from the starting point at Route 14A.

During seasons of normal rainfall this locale has an appeal for a wide variety of bird and wildlife. The trail offers opportunity for picnicking, exploring, and nature study. Carry a camera and/or binoculars and a magnifying glass. Wear waterproofed footwear, or carry rubbers, should you desire to investigate the swampy area where many shy and lovely flowers may be found.

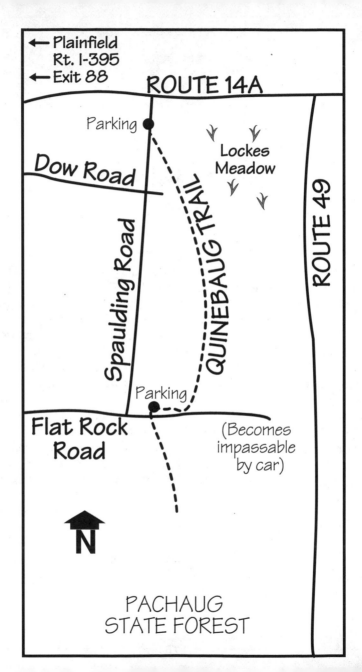

On these short walks it would seem, no matter what one's special interest may be, that wildflowers attract everyone's attention. Some of the specimens that one may encounter in season are hepatica, common and yellow violet, jack-in-the-pulpit, trillium, and possibly the semi-rare moccasin flower or lady's slipper.

It is estimated that there are some 500 odd species of native and introduced wildflowers in the northeastern part of the United States. Only the experts will know them all, but what a rewarding experience for the amateur when he is able to identify a flower by its name.

The *hepatica*, or liverleaf, prefers the leafmold soils of the high dry woodland, open woods, and forest slopes. The inconspicuous, fragile, single flowers, varying from lilac to bluish or white in color, defiantly push their way into the cold world while their hesitant leaves remain deeply hidden in their fuzzy wrappings, awaiting more favorable weather. How like their human counterparts! The frail and delicate-appearing stand the stress and hardships that often shatter their robust and hardy-looking companions.

The name *hepatica* comes from the Greek word meaning liver. The flower in all probability was given the name because its leaf resembles the outline of a liver. In consequence of this fancied likeness, the plant was used as a remedy for liver complaints, perhaps because omen-conscious peoples believed mother nature was indicating the use to which her creation might be applied.

You can enhance your pleasure of a walk in the woods and fields by learning the names and histories of the common flowers you come upon. One need not be a trained botanist to enjoy the flowers. There are numerous wildflower guides available at modest cost which can give the novice much help.

Note: The southern section of the Quinebaug Trail is described in Walk 60.

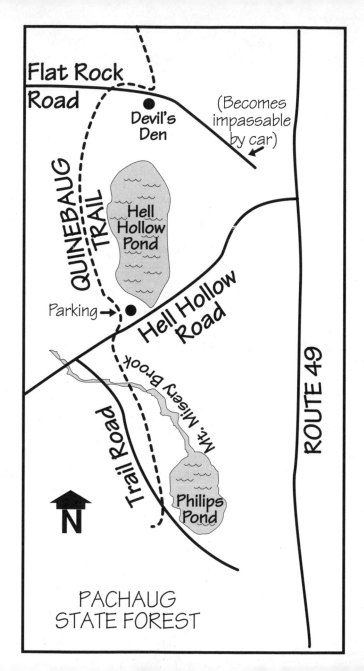

60

Hell Hollow

One of the easy and pleasant walks of the Connecticut Blue Trail System—despite its ominous, foreboding and inauspicious topographical names: Hell Hollow, Devil's Den, and Misery Brook—is on the Quinebaug Trail in the town of Voluntown.

The Quinebaug Trail is only 5.5 miles long, its southern section is in the town of Voluntown, its northern half in Plainfield. The Plainfield–Voluntown boundary is also the Windham–New London county line. The trail is mostly woods roads in the Pachaug State Forest.

To reach the Hell Hollow segment of the trail, follow road map routes to either the juncture of Routes 49 and 14A in Sterling or Route 49 with Routes 138 and 165 in Voluntown. From Route 14A follow Route 49 south approximately 3 miles to Hell Hollow Road. From the south and combined Routes 138 and 165, follow Route 49 north 5 miles to Hell Hollow Road.

Turn west onto Hell Hollow Road and follow it about 1.5 miles to where the Quinebaug Trail, indicated by blue-blazes, crosses the road. A large pond, through which Misery Brook flows, is on the north side of the road, .1 mile before the trail. Park your car off the traveled portion of highway.

Head north into the woods on the blue-blazed trail, which follows a woods road all the way to Flat Rock Road, about 1.5 miles from your parked car.

Turn right (east) onto Flat Rock Road and follow the blazed trail for approximately .4 mile to Devil's Den. The den is a mass of jumbled boulders and ledge just off the south shoulder of Flat Rock Road. Misery Brook flows past the east face of Devil's Den. This is an interesting area to explore.

The trail between Hell Hollow Road and Flat Rock Road follows high ground; deep, sunken Hell Hollow is below to the east, and still east of the hollow is a predominant high ridge. The woods road trail is a very easy one to hike, and there are numerous ledges off the main path that invite inspection.

From your parking spot on Hell Hollow Road, you can also head west on Hell Hollow, then south on the Quinebaug Trail or on Trail Road (dirt) for less than a mile to Philips Pond, a lovely spot with a waterfall and a picnic area.

If ever humans find paradise it will be in natural surroundings, not man-made plastic flowers, macadamized landscapes, or other artificial creations.

No other animal behaves as man does. Man kills not of necessity but just for the pleasure of destroying. We kill by violent and other means many living things: animals, birds, forests—some to complete extinction.

Only man wastes and destroys his gifts to such a degree that he is hard-pressed to find suitable ground in which to hide his garbage.

"Only man is vile." He leaves his litter, junked cars, beer cans, and rubbish wherever he roams, creating flaming swords of polluted land, water, and air with which he drives himself out of his gardens of Eden. No matter how many flaming swords are turned against him, he does not learn; he persists in befouling his Utopias.

Note: The northern section of the Quinebaug Trail is described in Walk 59.